THE INSTRUCTIONAL COACHING HANDBOOK

THE INSTRUCTIONAL COACHING HANDBOOK

200+ TROUBLESHOOTING STRATEGIES FOR SUCCESS

A. Keith Young | Angela Bell Julien | Tamarra Osborne

Arlington, Virginia USA

2800 Shirlington Rd., Suite 1001 • Arlington, VA 22206 USA
Phone: 800-933-2723 or 703-578-9600 • Fax: 703-575-5400
Website: www.ascd.org • Email: member@ascd.org
Author guidelines: www.ascd.org/write

Penny Reinart, *Chief Impact Officer;* Genny Ostertag, *Managing Director, Book Acqui-sitions and Editing;* Stephanie Bize, *Acquisitions Editor;* Mary Beth Nielsen, *Director, Book Editing;* Jamie Greene, *Senior Editor;* Thomas Lytle, *Creative Director;* Donald Ely, *Art Director;* Jennifer Knotts, *Graphic Designer;* Kelly Marshall, *Production Manager;* Christopher Logan, *Senior Production Specialist;* Valerie Younkin, *Senior Production Designer;* Shajuan Martin, *E-Publishing Specialist*

Copyright © 2023 ASCD. All rights reserved. It is illegal to reproduce copies of this work in print or electronic format (including reproductions displayed on a secure intranet or stored in a retrieval system or other electronic storage device from which copies can be made or displayed) without the prior written permission of the publisher. By purchasing only authorized electronic or print editions and not participating in or encouraging piracy of copyrighted materials, you support the rights of authors and publishers. Readers who wish to reproduce or republish excerpts of this work in print or electronic format may do so for a small fee by contacting the Copyright Clearance Center (CCC), 222 Rosewood Dr., Danvers, MA 01923, USA (phone: 978-750-8400; fax: 978-646-8600; web: www.copyright.com). To inquire about site licensing options or any other reuse, contact ASCD Permissions at www.ascd.org/permissions or permissions@ascd.org. For a list of vendors authorized to license ASCD ebooks to institutions, see www.ascd.org/epubs. Send translation inquiries to translations@ascd.org.

ASCD® is a registered trademark of Association for Supervision and Curriculum Devel-opment. All other trademarks contained in this book are the property of, and reserved by, their respective owners, and are used for editorial and informational purposes only. No such use should be construed to imply sponsorship or endorsement of the book by the respective owners.

All web links in this book are correct as of the publication date below but may have become inactive or otherwise modified since that time. If you notice a deactivated or changed link, please email books@ascd.org with the words "Link Update" in the subject line. In your message, please specify the web link, the book title, and the page number on which the link appears.

PAPERBACK ISBN: 978-1-4166-3171-2   ASCD product #123022   n3/23
PDF EBOOK ISBN: 978-1-4166-3172-9; see Books in Print for other formats.
Quantity discounts are available: email programteam@ascd.org or call 800-933-2723, ext. 5773, or 703-575-5773. For desk copies, go to www.ascd.org/deskcopy.

Library of Congress Cataloging-in-Publication Data is available for this title.
LCCN: 2022945993

30 29 28 27 26 25 24 23   2 3 4 5 6 7 8 9 10 11 12

THE INSTRUCTIONAL COACHING HANDBOOK

200+ TROUBLESHOOTING STRATEGIES FOR SUCCESS

Foreword

I wish I had had this book in the '70s when I started as an instructional coach. I would have learned that there is no singular best way to be in the role. Keith Young and his colleagues have captured the wisdom that "matching is the name of the game"—that selecting the best-fit approach across the directive to nondirective continuum is what skillful coaches learn how to do. They can diagnose the appropriate method to engage teachers with data and conduct conversations that are maximally helpful. They use the hallowed Situational Leadership framework for laying out the meaning of differentiated coaching.

No one is more versed in the coaching literature of this century or more respectful in crediting forebearers and fine minds in the field than Keith Young, Angela Bell Julien, and Tamarra Osborne. They have, indeed, created a synthesis of wise practitioners through the decades, but they have also added new dimensions to the field. In addition to the equity strand built into their concept of the coach's role, they place new emphasis on developing teacher belief about all students' capacity to learn despite the conditions of their birth. For leaders and coaches committed to equity, this book is a new window.

The Instructional Coaching Handbook also takes on the broadest range I have seen in areas that pertain to successful instruction, including coaching for SEL learning and for moving teachers toward mature professional stances of openness and humility about their own learning. The authors even include the critical area of coaching teachers to be effective team members. These are vital areas for professional growth well beyond traditional foci of problems of practice or implementation of new curricula. They address essential elements of professionalism that are as much a part of high-expertise teaching as knowing how to design high-quality lessons and plan effective implementation.

They also recognize that the most intensive and time-consuming coaching strategies revolve around planning and helping teachers understand the larger context and multiple factors involved in teaching day-to-day. Particularly interesting is the section on teacher assumptions or beliefs that interfere with their learning new behaviors. The authors' approach here shows the wisdom of and necessity for getting inside coachees' frames of reference.

This book is an encyclopedia of concrete, actionable tips and strategies for coaches, grouped in easy-to-find categories. Even though there is a theoretical coherence to the design of the book, there's nothing like concrete examples to illustrate an idea. One can open to almost any page and find something clearly understandable and empowering to do in practice.

There are no leaders or coaches who will *not* get new ideas from this carefully crafted book, no matter how experienced they are.

—Jon Saphier
Founder, Research for Better Teaching

Introduction

After decades of coaching teachers, coaches, and administrators, we set out in this book to provide the most helpful problem-solving strategies for coaching that we have used with and learned from educators across the United States and the world. Regularly, leaders request our advice on unique issues around coaching teachers. We took that advice, compiled it into common themes, and made each topic a chapter in this book. View the chapters as a menu of options; look up the general situation you've struggled with in coaching, and you'll find a list of ideas to try. The ideas are backed by research and the collective wisdom of coaches and administrators.

We provide a unique perspective. Not only do we train coaches, but we also require them to watch us lead conversations with teachers. Then we observe and provide feedback to them as they do likewise. In total, the three of us are in 2,500–3,000 classrooms each year across the United States and abroad, coaching teachers, training administrators, coaching coaches, or conducting model lessons. We sit on the floor of preschools and listen to coaches quietly give feedback to teachers about extending child language. You'll find us observing and advising administrators as they provide group feedback on a full day of classroom observations in a high school science department. We have witnessed significant gains in student academic and social-emotional skills as a result of our work and sometimes even outcomes that have catapulted schools through state-mandated school turnaround processes.

Further, we've done this work in diverse settings—in high schools in Arizona correctional facilities, in the homes of childcare providers in the Bay Area of Northern California, in remote schools on dirt roads serving Native American reservations, in public and private schools in Los Angeles and Chicago, and in schools in western Asia, Europe, and China. You might find Tamarra perched on a miniature chair in the backyard of a home childcare provider, whispering coaching points to teacher coaches. Angela has lost count of the high school science labs and culinary arts programs where she has modeled coaching for principals. Keith has even stood ankle-deep in mud for a coaching conversation with a horticulture teacher in a flooded Hawaiian taro field. (It was Hawaii, so there was no complaining.) Conducting and observing these coaching dialogues engendered much respect for those teachers, leaders, and coaches and the students in those educators' care.

How to Read This Book

We love practical information, and we intend this book to be a source for troubleshooting common coaching issues. Whether you're calibrating or recalibrating your coaching tactics, use this book much like an artist uses design principles or a chef uses spices from the pantry. Mix and match the strategies according to your leadership style, the needs of the student or teacher, and the demands of the curriculum. Identify a general issue—for example, the teacher doesn't embrace feedback, which would direct you to Chapter 5, "Coaching Openness to Feedback"; search through the suggestions; and try a few of the approaches with the teacher. If they don't work, redo the process using different strategies until you get a match that helps the teacher move forward in their practice.

Coaching Is a Conversation

Our firm belief is that *coaching is a work conversation with a clear goal*. Sometimes the teacher sets the goal, sometimes the coach sets the goal, and sometimes the teacher and coach mutually agree on the purpose. Regardless of the leader in this professional collaboration, the complex coaching relationship and the conversations that ensue are fraught with challenges. In *Masterful Coaching*, Hargrove (2008) described a coach as an individual who sees another's actions through focused observation and targeted listening. Hargrove noted that we often don't see the difference between our behaviors and our intentions; we intend or think we're doing one thing when we're actually doing something else. An effective coach helps bridge the gap between good intentions and actual objective results—and this happens through multiple, purposeful conversations.

This book is not about a new model of coaching. Instead, it's a resource that addresses the common obstacles that coaches face implementing any variety of coaching formats. We're big advocates of a blended or hybrid coaching model; that is, we pull the best strategies from what we know in the field of teacher coaching. We received training in several coaching frameworks: cognitive coaching (Costa et al., 2016); instructional coaching (Knight, 2018); the Danielson framework (Danielson, 2007); clinical supervision (Hunter, 1978, 1980); the Marzano teacher evaluation model (Marzano, 2013); Head Start's practice-based coaching (Head Start, 2020); Aguilar's *The Art of Coaching* (2013); Hasbrouck's *Student-Focused Coaching* (Hasbrouck, 2016; Hasbrouck & Denton, 2007); and administrator training (Saphier et al., 2018). Personal training from Robert Garmston, Jon Saphier, Robert Marzano, Elena Aguilar, and Bruce Wellman informs much of our work.

We've found that the most influential coaches are pros at switching stances according to the needs of the students in the classroom or the teacher's current skill set or disposition. Sometimes the coach needs to facilitate reflection with the teacher. After considering various probing questions, teachers may resolve their problem and come to a new understanding of their work. Other situations—such as a teacher with only a limited repertoire of strategies for changing a given practice—may require more direct intervention, with the coach becoming a teacher of the teacher. And regardless of how much a coach adores Dewey (1909/2019) or Schön (1983) and believes in the power of reflective thinking, some teachers are simply not very introspective, no matter how hard you nudge them to contemplate their practice. Finally, some teachers just need a coach to problem solve with them, vet ideas, or cosolve an issue.

This practice of switching coaching approaches echoes Blanchard's situational leadership theory (Hersey & Blanchard, 1969; Northouse, 2022), which describes how leaders or coaches change their guidance style to accommodate those they coach or lead. Elena Aguilar (2013) applied this theory in her coaching model, which advocates the importance of the coach switching from facilitative to directive coaching conversations. Earlier on, we encountered the same concept of moving between reflective and instructive coaching conversations in *Blended Coaching* (Bloom et al., 2005) and Coach for Success from WestEd (2016), where we trained and worked for years.

Coaching Is a Vision

In addition to situational leadership theory and the significance of moving among several coaching stances, we're also influenced by transformational leadership theory (Burns, 1978; Northouse, 2022). As coaches, we find it essential to maintain a vision of how teachers might change their attitudes, beliefs, and behaviors regarding solid teaching practices and dispositions. When we deploy more constructivist coaching activities with teachers, we often empower them to shift their attitudes and beliefs and come to new understandings about their students or their profession; at this point, we align with transformational leadership. We want teachers to expand what they believe students can learn, or we find ourselves acting as change agents in the coaching relationship to confront racist, sexist, or other harmful dispositions. In these moments and conversations, we seek to influence the whole person, not just teacher behaviors.

A Look at the Research on Coaching

In general, coaching has two or three goals. The first is often for the teacher to improve teaching practices, deploy evidence-based strategies, or implement a curriculum with fidelity (Knight, 2018; Snyder et al., 2015). Another more elusive goal is to improve student academic and social-emotional outcomes (Joyce & Showers, 1982, 2002; Snyder et al., 2015). All the while, the coach uses strategies of trust, rapport, and relationship building to maintain a collaborative partnership or alliance with the teacher (Snyder et al., 2015).

There's also the matter of coaching's effect on teacher practices, as opposed to student outcomes. Although Joyce and Showers (1982, 2002) found that training accompanied by coaching led to an 80 to 90 percent implementation of the training practices, more recent and extensive studies reveal that teacher practices experience more improvement than actual student outcomes. Kraft and colleagues' meta-analysis (2018) of 60 studies evaluating instructional coaching showed significant, positive effects of coaching on teachers' instructional practices (.49 standard deviation). However, the same research found that coaching had a more limited effect on student achievement (.18 standard deviation).

Research reveals that coaching influences other student outcomes. For example, Garet and colleagues (2016) found that coaching improved communication of conceptual understandings and solicitation of student thinking and resulted in enhanced student participation in mathematics. In another study, teachers involved in instructional coaching reduced the referrals of Black students for disciplinary action while increasing higher-level thinking and hypothesis generation in their lessons (Gregory et al., 2016). In sum, coaching has been found to directly or indirectly improve student achievement and social-emotional outcomes while, at the same time, improving teacher instructional practices (Garet et al., 2016; Gregory et al., 2016; Joyce & Showers, 1982, 2002; Knight, 2018; Kraft et al., 2018; Snyder et al., 2015).

The Research Behind Our Framework

In the course of our work, we have discovered a few potholes in productive coaching conversations on the road to successful outcomes. Coaches shared with us the most persistent trouble spots they encountered—and these trouble spots provided the outline for this book. Coaches frequently confronted challenges in coaching teachers in seven skills and dispositions: efficacy, equity, academic instruction, social-emotional instruction, openness to feedback, lesson planning, and team membership. This book devotes a chapter to each.

These seven skills and dispositions align with three prominent resources that underlie our framework. The first is Lisa Kim and colleagues (2019), who conducted a meta-analysis that examines teacher personality and educator effectiveness. The researchers reviewed 25 studies involving more than 6,000 individuals that defined *personality* as a psychological quality that influences behaviors, thoughts, and feelings. The researchers used the Big Five model to analyze the relationship between personality and teacher outcomes because it's the most prominently researched personality trait framework (John et al., 2008). The Big Five model uses common everyday language to describe people (Saucier & Goldberg, 1996) and sorts them into five domains:

- **Openness:** creative, curious, cultured
- **Conscientiousness:** organized, responsible, reliable
- **Extraversion:** sociable, assertive, energetic
- **Agreeableness:** kind, cooperative, trustful
- **Emotional stability:** calm, secure, unemotional

Kim and colleagues noted that four of the Big Five personality domains—openness, conscientiousness, extraversion, and emotional stability—were associated with teachers' ability to shape student outcomes and learning experiences. Agreeableness was not associated with teacher effectiveness.

John Hattie (2012) is our second important source. In *Visible Learning for Teachers*, he analyzed more than 800 meta-analyses involving 240 million students and proposed, among other findings, that students in classrooms with high-effect teachers gain approximately one year more of learning than students taught by low-effect teachers. Further, it is the *disposition* of exemplary teachers that caused high-effect teachers to outpace lower-effect teachers. Based on an extensive literature review, Hattie identified five dimensions of powerful teachers. They

- Identify the most powerful strategies to represent the content.
- Create an ideal classroom climate for learning.
- Monitor learning and provide explicit feedback.
- Believe all their students will reach high goals.
- Influence both academic and social-emotional student outcomes.

The third source underlying our work is Arthur Costa and colleagues (2016). In *Cognitive Coaching*, the researchers propose five educator *states of mind* that relate to the research findings from Hattie and Kim. These include

- **Consciousness:** knowing what I'm thinking as I work and reflecting on my actions
- **Skillfulness:** working toward excellence in my aptitude as an educator
- **Efficacy:** taking responsibility for the outcomes of my work
- **Flexibility:** considering options other than my own about my work
- **Interdependence:** knowing that we benefit from working in teams

An Overview of the Book

In Chapter 1, "Coaching Efficacy," we look at how teachers can embrace their power to improve student learning. Our recommendations help the coach help the teacher take ownership and feel and maintain the power inherent in their role as an educational leader.

In Chapter 2, "Coaching Equity," we consider the shared characteristics of teachers who confront and manage racism, sexism, and other systems of oppression while producing positive student outcomes. In this chapter, we offer approaches to influencing teacher mindsets so every student, regardless of background or identity, can achieve at high levels.

In Chapter 3, "Coaching Academic Instruction," we look at coaching teacher skills in academic delivery, likely the most common job of coaches. Here, we offer several strategies for coaching academic instruction in multiple content areas.

Chapter 4, "Coaching Social-Emotional Instruction," focuses on students' social and emotional concerns. This chapter offers effective strategies that target social and emotional learning.

In Chapter 5, "Coaching Openness to Feedback," we see that teachers who make significant gains with learners not only take feedback well but also often aggressively solicit feedback on their performance. Respecting the benefit of feedback is vital for a teacher working with a coach or supervisor. Chapter 5 offers the most extensive list of coaching strategies.

In Chapter 6, "Coaching Lesson Planning," we look at the attributes of teachers who carefully and thoroughly plan their lessons. Our most intensive and time-consuming coaching strategies focus on planning and helping teachers understand the larger context and multiple factors involved in day-to-day teaching. This chapter features strategies that will make the arduous work of coaching lesson planning most productive.

Chapter 7, "Coaching Team Membership," provides coaching advice to help teachers become cooperative team members. Some of our most creative work has been the result of bouncing ideas off others. Teachers skilled at working in teams bring a variety of skill sets to their work. Our recommendations in this chapter focus on helping teachers work productively with the other adults in the school.

In Chapter 8, "Tools That Will Help," we look at Young's Coaching Apps, which describe specific coaching dialogue frames and stems for the beginning, middle, and end of a coaching conversation. Also included are 18 coaching formats for when and where to conduct coaching.

Each chapter concludes with What It Looks Like in Practice, a section with a variety of implementation stories that connect with that chapter's coaching focus. We also offer several reflection questions at the end of each chapter.

We close our book with two appendices. Appendix A provides additional background on the research supporting Young's Coaching Apps, and Appendix B suggests some practical tools you can use to organize your coaching files and to script during classroom observations. Dive into a chapter that addresses an issue you are currently struggling with; scan for ideas that match your style, the teachers you coach, and your unique context; and start coaching!

1

Coaching Efficacy

When we consider efficacy, we like to turn to this definition (Costa et al., 2016): *efficacy is taking ownership of my work outcomes, good or bad.* Costa, Hattie (2012), and Kim and colleagues (2019) all found that influential teachers were highly efficacious, reflected on their actions, believed students could learn, and demonstrated conscientiousness. The Kim study also included conscientiousness as a positive indicator of teacher effectiveness because conscientious teachers have a strong drive and even a moral sense of duty. Hattie aligned teacher proficiency with efficacy, noting that effective teachers positively influence student outcomes, believe that all students can learn, monitor learning, provide explicit feedback during instruction, and identify powerful strategies to represent content. Exceptional instructors understand that their work has an impact; they know their power (Armor et al., 1976).

Our own experience has taught us that efficacious teachers possess a solid drive and an ethical obligation to their duties, are eager to engage in learning, and believe they can positively affect student learning. Efficacious teachers focus more on internal issues they can control, such as their time, skills, or expertise, and less on external factors outside their control, such as child attributes, family situations, systems, or students' socioeconomic status. These teachers focus on reaching goals despite obstacles; they feel they own the ultimate responsibility for student learning.

Let's look at this notion of efficacy in the context of the popular TV show *Chopped,* where competing chefs are tasked with making a delicious dish out of peculiar, mandatory ingredients. A chef lacking efficacy starts by blaming the ingredients or time allotment: "No one can transform a sickly sweet unicorn milkshake into dinner in 30 minutes!" Another competitor with significant efficacy confidently announces, "I know exactly where I'm going with this!" Similarly, efficacious teachers center their attention around arriving at educational objectives regardless of snags.

Let's look at various strategies that coaches can use to promote teacher efficacy.

Researcher	Effective Teacher Traits or Dispositions Related to Efficacy
Costa et al. (2016)	• Efficacy: seeks competence, mastery, control • Consciousness: monitors and reflects on thoughts and actions of self
Hattie (2012)	• Believes all students can reach the success criteria
Kim et al. (2019)	• Conscientiousness: ambitious, achievement focused, highly responsible

Strategies
1.1: Start Small

It's the coach's job to help the teacher take possession of the power inherent in an educator's job. As a coach, you must be tenacious until the teacher consistently demonstrates the smallest of steps. To keep a precise focus for your coaching work, *start small.*

The more the teacher struggles with an idea or a tactic, the more granular you want to make the action; go smaller and smaller, in terms of moves, until the teacher can complete the task proficiently. Then add additional or expanded steps.

For example, don't ask a teacher to "involve all students." That's far too vague. Instead, ask the teacher to have all students use gestures as they learn math vocabulary. For example, the teacher might ask all students to raise both arms to signal *parallel*. If only a few students gesture, ask the teacher to cue, "I need all hands in the air. Watch and follow." If some students are still not using the gestures, ask the teacher to recue: "*Almost* everyone has their hands in the air; now I need *everyone*." Start with one course or subject, one student, one practice, or one part of the curriculum, such as guided reading in language arts or concept development in mathematics.

1.2: Focus on One's Circle of Influence

Aguilar (2013) recommended highlighting three circles of influence in respect to students' lives and learning: one that the teacher maintains control over, one they can only influence, and one over which they have no control (see Figure 1.1). This strategy aims to help teachers focus on the first circle—on what they can actually control. For example, the teacher can control their words, actions, thoughts about a student, interactions or responses to situations in the classroom, the learning environment, activities, and so on. There's always something the teacher can control, even if the school, social, or home environments are chaotic and unmanageable.

When working with a team or person obsessed with an issue outside their control, use the image in Figure 1.2 to help them regain focus; this is another version of circles of influence. The larger area represents the general work goal or purpose. The smaller area at the bottom of the illustration represents the problem. Say something like this:

This larger area is our work, and this smaller area is the problem we have no control over right now. The problem is not off the page, and it does affect our work—but only to the slightest degree. Let's keep it in perspective and focus on the majority of our tasks that we can control.

Just acknowledging the issue and then placing it graphically into perspective may help the individual or group move forward.

Figure 1.1   Circles of Influence: Version 1

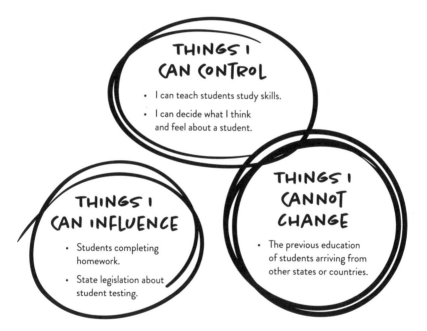

1.3: Ask the Five Whys

This activity, by Sakichi Toyoda (Ohno, 1988), gets at root causes for a belief and forces teachers to stay within their sphere of influence. The coach asks a series of five or more *why* questions about the teacher's situation to get at the cause of the problem. The questions help teachers arrive at broken processes or practices they had not previously considered; this is key to the process. Teachers may reply that there's "not enough time" to do the work they need to do, that "students have no prior skills," or that there's a "lack of social services" or "no administrator follow-through." These answers may be accurate, but they are, in most cases, outside the teacher's control. It's important to keep the conversation focused on rationales the teacher *can* control. Check out the implementation story "A Coach Uses the Five Whys" at the end of this chapter, which shows how one coach used this strategy with a teacher who was frustrated that some students weren't doing their homework.

Figure 1.2   Circles of Influence: Version 2

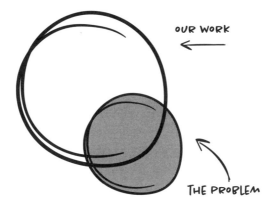

1.4: Keep the Teacher Focused

Some teachers may need help focusing during the coaching conversation. If so, avoid coaching during class time for a while, and only coach when the teacher is free of students. Ensure quiet and calm during the coaching session; there should be no phones pinging and no one walking in on the meeting. Provide the teacher with a notebook to record coaching points during their work with you. Review their coaching notes, and ask for a verbal summary of commitments at the end of each coaching session.

1.5: Express Your Belief in Capacity

Assure the teacher that you know they can learn complicated skills. You might say, "I know this is hard right now, but I'm confident you'll get this soon." If possible, remind them of something complex they completed in the past and were successful accomplishing.

1.6: Provide a Rationale

Continually remind the teacher of the primary concept or the big picture for why you're having them practice what they're doing. Explain how the small details that may feel overwhelming or confusing fit into the larger framework of a curriculum, student developmental needs, or an initiative.

Let's say a teacher balks at the idea of posting an objective or a learning target for the students to see. Instead of saying, "Because the research says so," it would be far more productive to cite specific researchers and studies. Explain the need for learners to know where they're going and when or how they'll be successful. Talk to the teacher about their own learning. How might knowing an expectation affect *their* ability to fulfill those expectations? For example, a teacher might have been asked to "write a lesson plan" without a template or an explanation of what the plan should include. How might a fuller explanation of expectations have helped the teacher be successful in the task? Explain that larger bodies of knowledge progress from a series of smaller daily targets. Talk about learning as being a set of concrete steps rather than a haphazard walk through a maze of mysteries.

1.7: Consider a Similar Problem

If the teacher feels overwhelmed or powerless implementing a new initiative, such as managing a student's behavior, ask them to focus on similar past issues: "Tell me about a time you solved a similar problem." The previous experience may or may not directly relate to the current one; capitalize on it either way. For example, if a new assessment is challenging, ask the teacher how they implemented a new curriculum or another assessment in the past. Did the teacher dedicate more time to study the curriculum? Did they create a more detailed calendar or set of checklists? Did they start with a tiny aspect of the new initiative before trying to deploy the entire framework? Have them focus on those strategies and use those past successful tactics to help manage the current issue.

1.8: Label Effort

Some teachers may not realize that their work did, indeed, produce the desired student result; in this case, articulate the connection for them. They may attribute their students' academic success to luck or actions unrelated to their teaching practices. Verbally correct their thinking each time they say something along the lines of "Oh, I got the good kids" or "That skill wasn't too challenging for them to learn." Highlight what they did or didn't do to produce the outcome. If needed, share the reading on attribution theory (Weiner, 1974), which describes how individuals perceive the causes of everyday experience as being either external or internal.

1.9: Point to Success Outside Teaching

Connect accomplishment in other areas to the task of teaching. Ask the teacher to describe something they're relatively successful at and continue to improve on (e.g., cooking, completing crossword puzzles, surfing, gaming, cleaning house). Next, ask them to recount exactly how they built their expertise and how they maintain that success. As they talk, note behaviors that influence their efficacy. When they finish, chart those behaviors, and ask them how they might replicate them in their classrooms.

1.10: Define *Efficacy*

Make sure the teacher is clear about the definition of *efficacy*. Help them go beyond the simple description of "efficacy as success." Move the conversation to words such as *innovate, evaluate*, and *effect* or to synonyms of those words. This may help the teacher see both a more specific and a broader view of the importance of being powerful and self-directed in their work.

1.11: Brainstorm

Problem solve together. Have the teacher use classroom data to capture successes, encourage them to talk about what has worked, and then ask them to think specifically about where their practice has *not* worked. Honor them as adult learners, and help them strategize ways to seek answers to problems (Knowles et al., 2020). (See more about adult learners in Chapter 7.) Brainstorm, and do cooperative research. To demonstrate this point, if the teacher remarks that they cannot get students to engage in meaningful conversations, ask which students, when, and concerning what topics. Which students *do* engage? What topics get them talking? What happened the one time the teacher had the greatest number of students talking? How can they replicate that? Get answers to the questions, analyze the data together, brainstorm solutions, and decide on a plan of action going forward.

1.12: Use Vertical Team Resources

Teachers often blame the grade level below or students' families for not helping students achieve. Instead, teach groups of teachers communication and goal-setting skills to gain collective efficacy. Lead teams of teachers through an *if/then* theory of action dealing with specific student achievement areas to reach consensus on non-negotiables at each level. According to Donohoo and Katz (2019), "Collective efficacy is strengthened when increases in student achievement are realized based on the sustained efforts of high-powered teams within schools" (p. 24). If grade bands work together to make a change, they see their collective effect.

Figure 1.3 shows sample prompts for an *if/then* theory of action. The first implementation story at the end of this chapter, "Collective Efficacy—Sharing the Load," shows how this idea worked with math teachers across schools in the same district.

Figure 1.3   Sample *If/Then* Prompts

1.13: Ask Reflective Questions

Ask open-ended questions to promote a teacher's capacity. Try these:

- What did you notice about your thinking once students showed you they understood the concept?
- The move was a powerful one! What were you thinking and feeling when that moment happened? How could you replicate it?
- That aspect of the lesson had a positive effect on student learning. How did you plan for it?
- What could you do to feel like you have more control over what you're doing?
- I noticed that these three things worked really well. Tell me, what was going through your mind when you did them?
- Here's where I started to lose track of where you were going with the lesson. What were your thoughts around this time?
- If you can't change this, how can you make peace with it?

1.14: Offer Recognition

Empower teachers with Hattie and Clarke's (2019) four-step research-based recognition strategy. The acknowledgment must describe

1. Precisely what the teacher did.
2. The effect of the action.
3. What the teacher needs to do next.
4. Why that practice is vital to continue.

Basing recognition on the practice's effect (step 2) and rationale (step 4) increases the chance the teacher will continue the approach in the future.

1.15: Decrease Personal Praise

Sometimes teachers change their practice only to please the leader or coach instead of basing change on best practices for student learning. To combat this, try to avoid saying, "I liked _____" or "I loved _____." This focuses the teacher on what makes you, the coach, happy, and it may disempower them if they overrely on your praise. Unfortunately, we've seen leaders with personal charm or charisma develop a cult of personality, where teachers only change their practice to make the coach happy. (For more on this, see the implementation story "The Cult of Personality" at the end of this chapter.) Instead, send the message that you want teachers to shift their work to align with best practices and the research base and to improve learning experiences for students—not to satisfy you.

That said, don't be afraid to be human and let the occasional "I liked that" slip out. There are times you'll witness something extraordinary, unique, or just beautifully crafted. On rare occasions, we've spontaneously led a coaching conversation with "I just loved how you _____!" because we were thrilled at what we witnessed. However, as soon as we did that, we mitigated the effect of possible overdependence on our personal praise by providing concrete rationales for why we were so joyful. The teacher's approach may have met a long-sought goal, the students may have immediately and positively responded, the lesson may have been a picture-perfect reflection of high-quality research, or the teacher may have skillfully implemented a complex approach.

1.16: Make a Checklist

In today's world, our knowledge base often exceeds our capacity to hold in our heads all the pertinent information required for the complex task of teaching; in this case, a checklist may be a teacher's best friend. In *The Checklist Manifesto*, Gawande (2011) debunks the myth that professionals carry in their heads all the knowledge needed for their discipline. Most professionals, including surgeons, pilots, investment bankers, and others, reference multiple checklists for routine practices. To help teachers implement a technique, whether the teachers are new, struggling, or experienced, create a simple list of steps. Try to keep the number of steps to around four (Cowan, 2000). Revise and revisit the steps as needed.

1.17: Be Trauma Informed

Many adults experienced trauma and, as a result, may not feel they maintain much power over their work environment. Using the five principles of trauma-informed care (Institute on Trauma and Trauma-Informed Care, 2022), check your coaching for the following attributes:

1. **Safety.** Ensure physical and emotional safety. Offer to provide one-on-one coaching in a private office if needed. Ask teachers for their permission before coaching them live in the classroom or in front of others. Don't share your conversations with others, and be clear from the beginning of the relationship who has access—a supervisor, an administrator, or someone else—to the content of coaching conversations.

2. **Choice.** When possible, provide choices. When and where would the teacher prefer coaching? (See Chapter 8 for 18 options for places and times for coaching.) Even if a teacher has no choice in whether or not they engage in coaching, you can still offer some degree of choice during the coaching process. In addition to being a tenet of trauma-informed practice, having a choice is crucial when dealing with adult learners and should be part of your regular coaching practice (Knowles et al., 2020). Be clear about agreements for action at the end of coaching talks. Provide a variety of ways that

the teacher might accomplish a given strategy or approach or offer a selection of strategies to solve an issue.

3. **Collaboration.** This book is full of strategies for brainstorming or collaborating about ideas for improving teacher practices; use those tactics regularly. Be clear about your coaching disposition: when you plan to be more direct and why, when you want to collaborate through reflection or problem solving, and so on. Simply tell the teacher which coaching approach you're taking; we regularly rotate among four approaches—appreciating, brainstorming, instructing, and reflecting. Ask the teacher for feedback on your coaching skills and the coaching process.

4. **Trustworthiness.** Be clear about the norms or expectations of the coaching process, and don't violate them. *Blended Coaching* (Bloom et al., 2005) even recommends printing out agreements between the coach and teacher for both to sign, lending more formality to coaching expectations. Set clear boundaries for discussion topics. Chapter 5 offers additional ideas about managing professional and private topics in coaching.

5. **Empowerment.** Focus on strategies that empower the teacher while empowering the students. Appreciate teacher efforts at improvement and self-examination.

1.18: Focus on Big Picture/Little Picture Goals

Help the teacher articulate how the small activity they're planning directly relates to supporting the larger learning goal for the students. Ask the teacher, "Where are you going with this skill in relation to the standard or benchmark? More importantly, where is the student going?" Sometimes it's easy to get caught up in planning a series of learning activities or events and to forget the end goal or target. Help the teacher keep this in mind. Figure 1.4 shows how you can illustrate this point with the teacher.

Figure 1.4 Big Picture, Little Picture Goals

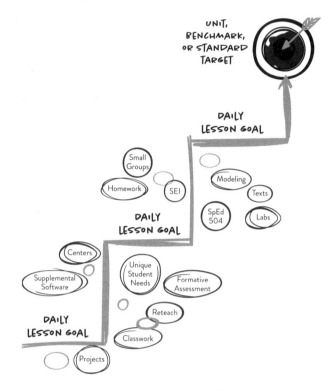

1.19: Ensure Teachers Know Multiple Names for the Same Concept

Like many fields, education uses numerous terms to describe a concept or an idea. Teachers should learn other common words for a tactic they're using in their current school or curriculum. In that case, they're more likely to comprehend the rationale behind the strategy and use it even if they move to another program, city, or district. For example, if a high school we worked with called an activator a *bell activity*, we made sure the teachers knew the crucial attributes of an activator according to the research and all the possible labels for that activator, such as a *starter activity*, a *do-now*, a *warm-up,* or *connecting to prior knowledge.* We wanted the teachers to focus on the concept behind the required activity, and we wanted them empowered regardless of their locale.

1.20: Coach Teachers to Curate

Teach teachers to be curators of instructional skills, examples, projects, and assignments that address the most demanding learning hurdles for their students. Working with teachers across the United States and internationally, we frequently ask for a list of the most challenging topics to teach for each grade level, age group, or course. Inevitably, teachers list similar issues regardless of their locale or population. Here are a few examples:

- Inferencing in elementary reading
- The conceptual understanding of zero
- Two-digit addition in 2nd grade
- Literary analysis in high school
- Missing math foundation skills at multiple levels
- The schwa sound in phonics
- Accessing grade-level texts when reading comprehension is low
- Transitions in classroom management
- Social-emotional skills at multiple levels
- Distinguishing between reality and fantasy in kindergarten
- The political concept of left, right, and center in high school government
- Writing up the results of a mixed-methods approach at the university level

As coaches, it's essential to know that every grade or course houses a handful of topics that are quagmires instructionally. Learn what the pitfall issues are, collect strategies for teaching those topics, and clarify for teachers the importance of collecting ideas for their subject or age group. Do teachers need a dozen ways to teach every skill or concept in their curriculum? No. However, they might need 8–10 good ideas to teach the most complex standards. Do this, and you'll empower them for the remainder of their careers.

1.21: Discuss the Benefits of Stress

Take a page from *The Upside of Stress* (McGonigal, 2015) and discuss the benefits of stress with the teacher. When some people feel stressed, they lose their sense of power or efficacy. McGonigal reported work as one of the four most significant sources of stress; people who thought stress wasn't harmful were less likely to die from stress-related illness. Stress might signal a need to change something, not everything; it may mean that we need to learn something new or that we shouldn't assume everything is wrong with our job. Help the teacher explore precise stress points about their work, discuss what they do and don't have control over, and help them learn new tactics for managing stress.

1.22: Promote an Outward Mindset

According to the Arbinger Institute (2016), keeping an *outward mindset* asserts that you will meet your own needs, challenges, and objectives—once you meet those of others. When working with a teacher, keep a log of what they tell you about their needs, challenges, and ideals. Also, observe what the teacher doesn't voice but conveys through actions. For example, the teacher may not remark that some students are not capable learners, but they then relegate some pupils to drilling basic skills while offering others higher-level thinking activities. Contemplate each concern and prepare to meet that teacher's needs so they can meet their students' needs. For example, the teacher might make errors as they teach a math lesson and become frustrated because they cannot teach a new curriculum;

this may manifest as anger or doubt about the curriculum's worth. The teacher might mention that they're restricted by the curriculum or that they cannot teach the topics that would truly reach their students of color; this attitude may manifest as a lack of confidence. Teachers need to recognize and strive for their *own* genius every day.

Assure the teacher that with a few changes in practice and a bit of ingenuity, they *can* become proficient. Spend time with them going over the next lesson or chapter, and collaboratively (through thinking aloud) help them make sense of the material and practice their examples for the class. Ask good questions that the students might ask, and help prepare answers. Building the teacher's skills will help cultivate their genius within themselves, leading to confidence, self-reliance, and empowerment in the classroom for everyone (Muhammad, 2020).

1.23: Foster Positive Beliefs About Power

If you find that the teacher's beliefs about power hinder their work, ask, "What do you believe about your ability to influence student learning?" "Do you believe children are born inherently bad?" "Do you think children prefer gendered activities when they come out of the womb?" "Do you think some people are naturally mathematically inclined and others are not?" "Do you believe students of marginalized communities (such as Black or Latinx students) are capable of success?" Explore the relationship between the teacher's beliefs about their power and the inherent power they believe students hold. Surface these beliefs—examine them, nudge them, and study why the idea is there. If you fail to address foundational issues regarding teaching and learning, you will not be effective. It's incumbent on the coach to lead the teacher to question these beliefs about power—the teacher's power as well as the student's—that hinder their ability to influence learning.

1.24: Make the Most of Grade-Level or Content Team Expertise

Coaching is often a one-to-one experience, but team coaching can be powerful and build collective efficacy. For example, suppose you observe a group of teachers teaching the same lesson at the same grade level, and you notice similar misconceptions, or maybe one teacher is having a more significant effect on student learning. In that case, bring them together for coaching. Questions such as "What effect did the lesson have on struggling learners?" or "What questions did you ask, and how did students answer?" can help them reflect as a team. You can share the similarities and differences you noted. If the team has a strong relationship, you can use the expertise of one to lift the others. All participants must understand that the purpose is to learn from one another and the coach in team coaching.

What It Looks Like in Practice

Collective Efficacy—Sharing the Load

Focus Strategies:
- Use vertical team resources
- Make the most of grade-level or content team expertise

Angela and Keith worked with high school math teachers who faced the possibility of being reassigned because of low student test scores. After spending some time with the teachers, we realized their collective efficacy was nonexistent. They believed that the low scores were due to high mobility in the school and district. After some research, we found that students who actually had been in the district the longest were failing at the highest rates. Also, the teachers believed that the elementary and middle schools were not doing their part to prepare students. After much data analysis, the teachers agreed to a multigrade meeting (grades 4–10) to determine how to make students more successful.

We brought together representatives from every grade level in the feeder system to address the following question: *How do we grow students who can master the standards of Algebra I by the end of 9th grade?* The discussion revealed numerous misconceptions, and much time was spent on topics that didn't move students toward successful progression through upcoming grades. But when we focused on *if/then* scenarios—that is, creating a set of nonnegotiables for each grade—great things happened. For example, "If 4th graders master _____, then 5th graders can _____."

The most exciting part of the first workday occurred when teachers left, stating that what they had described was doable. They had a plan to work together to be successful at each grade level. The act of paring down what students needed to learn, sharing the load, and believing that they could accomplish it was dynamic. Scores began to climb the first year afterward and continued steadily after that. We focused on the coaching strategies *make the most of grade-level or content team expertise* and *use vertical team resources* to make this result happen.

A Coach Uses the Five Whys

Focus Strategy:
- Ask the five whys

Here's an example of how a coach can use the tactic *ask the five whys*. A teacher was concerned that students weren't doing their homework. Here's what the conversation between coach and teacher looked like:

Coach: *Why* is this a problem?

Teacher: The students lose points, and it lowers their grades.

Coach: *Why* do they lose points for not doing their homework?

Teacher: [after a long pause] They need to do their homework to practice what they're learning. We don't have time to do that during the school day.

Coach: Let me take a quick sidetrack. How do you know they're ready to practice?

Teacher: What do you mean?

Coach: Have they all mastered the new learning well enough to practice it on their own?

Teacher: Well, not all of them.

Coach: What if they practice it wrong?

Teacher: I'll correct it with them in the morning.

Coach: OK, back to the whys. *Why* do you have students practice before they're ready?

Teacher: Well, parents should help; that should be their responsibility.

Coach: Let's remember to stay in your sphere of influence—what *you* control. Why do you have students practice before they're ready?

Teacher: Then I can correct what they do wrong. But they aren't doing their homework, so I don't get to show them what they've done wrong. Or I don't catch each student's errors on my own before the test. Then they take the test and don't do well, and I have to teach the same thing repeatedly.

Coach: *Why* do they fail?

Teacher: Because they don't practice.

Coach: Staying in your sphere of influence, *why* don't they practice?

Teacher: Because I don't build practice time into my lessons.

Coach: We've found a root cause: students need to practice *with you* first.

The Cult of Personality

 Focus Strategies:
- Decrease personal praise
- Do this every day, all the time (see Chapter 3)

One turnaround principal that Keith coached was highly charismatic and charming. Teachers in that low-performing school were quickly able to achieve full staff delivery of multiple strategies. All the while, the school made sharp gains in student achievement. Then the charismatic principal left to go to a different school, and Keith coached the new principal.

Lo and behold, once the charming principal left, the staff regressed on their embrace of best practices. When Keith confronted the former principal about this state of affairs, he learned that the principal had used personality to gain cooperation from the former staff. It was a practice they had used in the past, even though Keith had warned them about creating change based solely on personality. Still, the principal had no idea the staff were so profoundly motivated by their friendship and personality skills. They needed to work on the strategy *decrease personal praise*. The charismatic principal promptly stopped this habit in their current school.

The new principal started sending these messages to staff: "You need to use these practices every day—all the time—for the remainder of your career. Students need to encounter these strategies every single day in every single lesson, not just when I'm in the room." (We highlight this strategy *do this every day, all the time* in Chapter 3.) With a switch to this consistent messaging, the new administrator and school coaches led the staff to fully implement the necessary practices, and student outcomes steadily increased. But the lesson remains: don't overdepend on personal praise and personality to move best practices into place for students.

The Hula Hoop

 Focus Strategy:

- Coach teachers to curate

Tamarra observed an unforgettable example of the strategy *coach teachers to curate* when working in a preschool with teachers of students with autism. One challenge that teachers had in the school was getting students to come to them when requested. A student on the playground would frequently run in the other direction or simply refuse to move when prompted to return to class. Savvy teachers knew that the student would run if the teacher ran after them, and it became a game for the student, reinforcing the running behavior.

Seasoned teachers do otherwise. They get to know the student and what the student likes. With that knowledge, they use items or statements to attract the student. Sometimes the teacher will put a student's favorite toy in their apron and take it out and show the student, saying, "Come help take your little elephant into the classroom. Let's go." Or the teacher might announce that the class will sing the student's favorite song during circle time—once everyone's back inside. Many teachers trade favorite strategies with one another, and the coaches take part in countless conversations working on this skill set of "attracting, not chasing."

One sunny day in Los Angeles, Tamarra stood with several experienced teachers, coaches, and administrators during the transition from the playground to the classroom. A student teacher called a preschooler with autism to come inside, and, sure enough, the student ran to the far side of the playground. The novice teacher reached over, picked up a hula hoop, and hurled it toward the student, yelling,

"Benni, bring me my hula hoop!" Like a spring, the student shot after the rolling hoop, sprinted it back, grabbed the teacher's hand, and took them both inside the classroom. All the old pros stood gobsmacked. When they asked the student teacher why they did that, they replied, "You told me not to chase the kids, so I just grabbed something for Benni to catch." Every single experienced teacher, coach, and administrator promptly wrote down the hula hoop strategy. Powerful educators know the significance of curating strategies for challenging skills, and that surely was a stunning one we witnessed that day.

Coaches, Consider This...

- What general challenges do you face coaching teacher efficacy?
- Which strategies from this chapter will you experiment with and why?
- After experimenting, come back here and jot down your thoughts:
  » These are the strategies I tried:

  » Here's what happened:

2

Coaching Equity

As reported by Hattie (2012), teachers who substantially affect student learning emphatically accept that every student can reach challenging goals. Kim and colleagues (2019) identified conscientiousness and moral responsibility as contributing to equitable practices; outstanding teachers commit to ensuring that historically low-performing students meet demanding standards. Further, Costa and colleagues (2016) noted efficacy and skillfulness as essential for teachers to maintain equitable practices.

Unfortunately, coaches work with a few educators who believe that race, ethnicity, gender, socioeconomic status, language ability, disability, and sexual identity are severe impediments to high academic or social-emotional learning. This chapter offers numerous strategies for advocating for, understanding, and recognizing all students' unique and valuable aspects.

Researcher	Effective Teacher Traits or Dispositions Related to Equity
Hattie (2012)	• Creates an optimal climate for learning

Researcher	Effective Teacher Traits or Dispositions Related to Equity
Hattie (2012) (*continued*)	• Believes all students can reach the success criteria • Influences a wide range of student outcomes not solely limited to test scores
Kim et al. (2019)	• Conscientiousness: achievement focused, highly responsible

Strategies

2.1: Start Small

Start small to keep from overwhelming a teacher. Instead of tackling all students who are not succeeding in a class, ask the teacher to focus on one or two at first. Have the teacher experience success with a couple of students; they can then move to others in the class who are part of the same subpopulation and who are not achieving or receiving equitable instruction. You might then start discussions about systemic inequities and how those inequities show up in classrooms.

2.2: Try Future Casting

If you've done a great deal of talking and writing to communicate with a teacher and you've only seen minimal results, try *future casting*, a guided imagery strategy from Rob Bocchino (1999) that focuses on the kinesthetic or visual. Sometimes a complete shift in the coaching approach can jumpstart change—especially change that targets core values and assumptions.

A version of this process first appeared in Bocchino's book *Emotional Literacy* (1999). Some of us engaged in this activity in workshops with Rob around the same time. Years later, we ran across a similar approach in *Results Coaching* (Kee et al., 2010). The coach introduces the activity and calls out the following prompts as the teacher physically responds, moving around the room:

1. Select a goal for the student or students who are not performing well, either academically or socially. You don't have to share the goal, but you may if you want to.

2. Stand up and throw out a mental timeline in front of you. Imagine the timeline is as long as it takes to reach your goal but that it's contained within the room. The end of the timeline is where you accomplish your vision.

3. Walk to the end of the timeline. Step outside the area delineating the achieved goal. Describe it. What does it sound like? What does it look like? Describe it in third person.

4. Step back into the vision area and describe what you feel and see.

5. Go back to the start of the timeline. Look up the timeline to your vision at the end. What forces are present to help you reach that vision (your determination, skills, dispositions, people, and so on)? What influences hinder you? What do you need to turn that vision into reality? What first actions do you need to take?

6. Walk forward a bit on the timeline to a date a few months or weeks from the present. Tell yourself how you'll feel if you haven't acted on your vision. How does that feel?

7. Go past the completed vision, beyond the end of your timeline. Turn around and look back. You're in a position of wisdom. You maintain a new, wiser perspective. What message of wisdom would you send to your past self at the beginning of the timeline? Write that down and use it when you meet hurdles on the road to your vision.

Teachers may take reflective notes as they move through the process or write a reaction following the activity. By asking the teacher to use their imagination and physically move around, the facilitator attempts to get the teacher to experience the issue from another perspective and perhaps see a different or more definitive outcome. Occasionally, a teacher may become emotional as a result of the activity. It might touch places in the heart that multiple conversations never reach. Figure 2.1 illustrates the process.

Figure 2.1 Future Casting

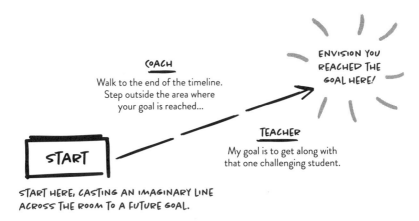

2.3: Share Social Data (Stories)

Share stories or show how other people succeeded with the same types of students. Use your anecdotes of accomplishments and gather accounts from others you work with and read about. Write down or keep a file of these accounts. Pull them out and use them as needed.

It's one thing to say that "all students can learn," citing the research that supports that claim. On the other hand, it's potent to recount examples of teachers who produced student learning when the odds seemed stacked against them. People often recall stories more than they do research specifics; the stories help them create a vision of what might be in their situation. We call sharing stories *social data* because it sounds more formal and prompts the coach to remember that multiple forms of data can move people forward.

2.4: Offer Video Examples

Visible examples are transformative because they provide a concrete picture of potential when it's hard to see a different future with students. Locate videos about high-performing schools with significant percentages of high-needs students where teachers produced successful student outcomes from marginalized communities. Again, teachers often remember your visual images and anecdotes more than the research supporting your point.

2.5: Engage in Difficult Conversations

Make a plan to sit down and discuss a challenging topic with the teacher. Classroom data may show that the teacher encourages certain students to do most of the talking in the classroom while students of color play only supporting roles during discussion. Draft the conversation beforehand, or jot down notes if you're unaccustomed to this or nervous. We recommend the following process for preparing for the conversation, which we adapted from our own experience and from insights from several authors (Aguilar, 2013, 2016; Anderson & Buchko, 2016; Sujansky & Ferri-Reed, 2009; Von Bergen et al., 2014):

- Write down the belief or beliefs you need to confront. Record practices, statements, data, and activities you witnessed that reveal the teacher's conviction. Be precise and only write down data points. Data can include your observation notes, student survey reports, teacher quotes, achievement data, and so on.

- Based on your data and experience, write down what you believe is the rationale behind this teacher's belief. Why do you think the teacher holds this belief?
- Write down why this belief conflicts with your opinions about students, people in general, teaching, or education.
- Record what you believe are reasonable practices and beliefs that could be replacement behaviors. Do you have any examples or research to back up your ideas? Write them down. Could you illustrate or role-play the replacement behaviors if needed? Sometimes a clear graphic communicates more than a lot of words.
- Plan who you want in the discussion—for example, an advocate, a defender, a compassionate listener, an attentive audience, someone who is open to alternative points of view, someone who is mindful, or an instructor. Ensure that you have a clear, positive intention behind confronting the teacher.
- List all the arguments the teacher may make against your suggestion. Then, mentally or in writing, prepare a defense for each point.
- Be ready for the teacher to disclose unknowns during the discussion. Perhaps someone *did* tell them to do what you're highlighting, or they may explain that they're managing a challenging medical or family issue. Listen carefully, and be ready to acknowledge or address those issues if needed. Regardless of what the teacher discloses, don't be tempted to mitigate your message. If this issue is significant enough for you to plan this discussion, then this is not the time to excuse the behavior due to personal circumstances. You'll likely think of others who manage similar issues and still exhibit the behavior or belief you're advocating.
- What are your best wishes and greatest fears for the discussion? Can you live with those potential outcomes?

- How might you request that the teacher change their behavior? What evidence will you both agree to look at? Set a timeline for this to occur and a date to revisit the issue soon.

If you're still unsteady about the conversation after your writing session, find a trusted colleague or friend for role-playing the conversation. We've done this for coaches, administrators, directors, and superintendents. Each time, the person who practiced with us was relieved and more confident leading the conversation.

2.6: Teach Attribution Theory and Mindset Tenets

Teach the teacher about the expandable nature of intelligence and to what successful learners attribute their success (Good et al., 2003; Saphier, 2017; Saphier et al., 2018; Weiner, 1974). Ensure the teacher understands that science is clear that intelligence is flexible and expandable; it is *not* cemented from birth. In addition, explain Dweck's (2016) principles about the importance of mistakes, learning, growing skills, and self-reflection. Coaches tell us that they frequently encounter teachers unfamiliar with these basic tenets of education.

2.7: Conduct a 30-Day Experiment

Encourage the teacher to experiment for 30 days with specific academic support, consistently, for one of their low-achieving students—a student they doubt can perform at a higher level. We've worked with teachers over the years to complete this activity multiple times. Some teachers provide extra daily tutoring for the student, others pull the student into small groups during each lesson for reteaching, and others target the student with daily explicit oral or written feedback. Almost without exception, if the teacher takes the challenge earnestly, the student improves. This approach is a practical way to show teachers that their expectations, when diligently deployed, change students.

2.8: Hold High Expectations of Students

Another strategy similar to the 30-day experiment involves the teacher repeatedly stating three crucial messages to a target student about their expectations. This approach comes from Saphier and colleagues (2018). For about four weeks and *every single day*, the teacher finds creative ways to voice three affirmations, adapted here, to the student:

- Say, *"This is important."* Establish the significance of the learning. For example, "You need to be able to do this to be successful in the lab work next week" or "This will empower you in all other classes, guaranteed."
- Say, *"You can do it."* Communicate the universal applicability of the skills or concept with comments like "No one fell out of the womb being able to create Excel spreadsheets or speak Arabic" or "Everybody can learn it; you can, too."
- Say, *"I'm not going to give up on you."* Tell the student, "My work is to help you until the last day you're under my professional care."

At the midway and endpoints of the 30 days, debrief the results with the teacher. Did the student change as a result of the intervention? Why or why not? Did the teacher learn anything about stereotypes of students who look like or act similarly to this student?

2.9: Encourage Teachers to Be Warm Demanders

Teachers who are warm demanders expect great things from their students. These teachers hold high academic and social standards while showing students care and love. Such teachers convince students of their academic and social brilliance and firmly guide them to learn in a structured environment (Delpit, 2012; Kleinfeld, 1975). Some teachers believe they have to be strict to keep high standards or overly friendly to demonstrate care; in fact, the research reveals they can combine both approaches. Teach the teacher this concept.

Some teachers believe that dual-language learners need simplified work below grade level. Show them the writing or reading rubric their state uses for dual-language learners. They will find high expectations. Have them consider what students that age care about, think about, and hold interest in. Help them realize that their dual-language learners are no different. Support teachers in developing strategies that enable dual-language learners to think at appropriate levels (by adding visuals or audio or by breaking the learning into smaller chunks) and continually expand their language skills.

2.10: Clarify There Are No "Small Problems"

If you raise an issue and the teacher responds that it's only a small problem, that only one or two students are affected, consider responding with something like "For those one or two students, the problem is not small." Show the teacher how interventions resolved student problems in significant ways. Ensuring that the student enters the right high school course, knows phonics skills, or embraces the tiniest bit of hope from a teacher may be life-changing for that student. Too often, those "one or two" are dual-language learners or special education students. Ask the teacher to examine the "one or two" and consider the effect on those students. What if they're affected in every learning situation every day? Provide novice teachers with tools to help those students. For more veteran teachers, brainstorm how they would teach if *all* their students were "the one or two."

2.11: Define a Belief

Some coaches find it difficult to disagree with teachers about their beliefs because they think they're somehow sacrosanct and immutable. Beliefs, however, change all the time. A belief is just a repeated thought about something considered absolute. If I can change my thoughts, I can change my belief, regardless of how long or how firmly I held the idea. Remind the teacher that views may shift; some opinions change quickly, some may take years to shift, and some may never change. If you find a teacher's belief harms students— such as "Some of my students just can't do what I expect of them"— then it's incumbent on you to nudge or confront the teacher. Help them develop an assets-based mantra instead, such as "I want to see what they can do—how close might they get?"

2.12: Use Academic Excellence Slogans

Give the teacher scripts for excellence to use with student populations that have traditionally been disempowered (Muhammad, 2020). Ask the teacher to pepper phrases such as the following throughout their verbal interactions with students:

- "Black academic excellence"
- "Mexican American innovation"
- "You're going to and through college."
- "Brilliant female scientists"
- "America's innovative founding immigrants"

2.13: Consider All Aspects of Students as Learners

Do you work with teachers who are hijacking their critical thinking with an obsession over student labels? Have teachers select three students to think about deeply. Then have them consider the following questions: What does *special education student* mean to you? What are other, more descriptive terms for a student labeled as a *slow starter*? For students labeled as *low performers* or *high performers*, what skills do those students have or not have? Can a student be *low* in decoding but *high* in making inferences? What do you mean by *creativity,* and how do you see that in that student? Does the student learn through careful reading of directions or through social interaction with you or their peers? Answer these questions with the teacher and make a plan for equitable instruction that considers *all* aspects of students as learners—not just how schooling labeled them.

2.14: Review Grading Practices

Ask the teacher how their grades reflect or depict learning. How does the teacher communicate their understanding of "grades and learning" to students? What is the difference between academic learning and completing assignments? Take a close look at those students who are receiving high and low grades. Have a frank discussion with the teacher about whether the high performers look, learn, act, or speak *like the teacher*. How is the teacher assessing? What other forms of assessment might more accurately measure learning for all students? Check out the book *Grading for Equity* by Joe Feldman (2018) for more ideas on this topic.

2.15: Observe Student Academic Thinking

While observing the teacher, note each student who demonstrates academic thinking (beyond recall). Record when and what thinking occurred and explain why you're labeling evidence as you are. Share your notes with the teacher. If they see a disparity between who is and isn't displaying academic thinking, discuss strategies. If the teacher doesn't recognize that only a few students are doing the thinking (or that the teacher is doing all the thinking), share with them a thinking routine such as Headlines, where students write a headline summary of the text and share it with a partner to reveal their thinking. This and other tactics are found in *Making Thinking Visible* (Ritchart et al., 2011).

2.16: Encourage Multidimensional Views of Students

Get teachers to challenge their comfort zone. Point out the positive aspects of the student's behavior or a different view of the student: "Yes, that student is defiant. At the same time, well-respected rebels founded our nation. Let's troubleshoot how we might harness that independent nature toward our learning goals." A coach's gift to the coaching relationship is promoting another view of a student or a situation. Sometimes the teacher needs to consider another perspective to determine how they might best approach that student.

2.17: Conduct an Independent-Dependent Learner Audit

When observing in a classroom, take careful notes concerning which students the teacher asks to think at higher depth-of-knowledge (DOK) levels (Webb, 2002, 2007). Which students have to find their answers and defend them with text or evidence? Who are given leadership roles in the class? Likewise, note students who spend most of their time doing drills, answering basic recall or DOK 1 questions, or copying from the teacher's or someone else's work. Discuss your evidence with the teacher. Ask the teacher if these tactics were conscious decisions. If so, why? This tactic is adapted from *Culturally Responsive Teaching and the Brain* (Hammond, 2015).

2.18: Propose a Book or Resource Study

Engage the teacher in intensive study of equity and antiracist practices. Have the teacher consider questions from study guidelines for the book in question. As they read, check in to talk about their learning and any questions they have. Consider these recent or recently revised titles:

- *A Race Is a Nice Thing to Have: A Guide to Being a White Person or Understanding the White Persons in Your Life* by Janet E. Helms (2019)
- *Advancing Equity in Early Childhood Education: A Position Statement of the National Association for the Education of Young Children* by NAEYC (2019)
- *Biased: Uncovering the Hidden Prejudice That Shapes What We See, Think, and Do* by Jennifer L. Eberhardt (2019)
- *Building a Movement to End the New Jim Crow: An Organizing Guide* by Daniel Hunter (2015)
- *Cultivating Genius: An Equity Framework for Culturally and Historically Responsive Literacy* by Gholdy Muhammad (2020)
- *Culturally Relevant Pedagogy: Asking a Different Question* by Gloria Ladson-Billings (2021)
- *Culturally Responsive Teaching and the Brain: Promoting Authentic Engagement and Rigor Among Culturally and Linguistically Diverse Students* by Zaretta Hammond (2015)
- *For White Folks Who Teach in the Hood... and the Rest of Y'all Too: Reality Pedagogy and Urban Education* by Christopher Emdin (2016)
- *Grading for Equity: What It Is, Why It Matters, and How It Can Transform Schools and Classrooms* by Joe Feldman (2018)
- *High Expectations Teaching: How We Persuade Students to Believe and Act on "Smart Is Something You Can Get"* by Jon Saphier (2017)

- *How to Be an Antiracist* by Ibram X. Kendi (2019)
- *Me and White Supremacy: Combat Racism, Change the World, and Become a Good Ancestor* by Layla F. Saad (2020)
- *"Multiplication Is for White People": Raising Expectations for Other People's Children* by Lisa Delpit (2012). (This is written for all educators; it isn't just a book about teaching math.)
- *The New Jim Crow: Mass Incarceration in the Age of Color-blindness* by Michelle Alexander (2020)
- *The New Jim Crow Study Guide and Call to Action* by the Veterans of Hope Project (2013)
- *Race Talk and the Conspiracy of Silence: Understanding and Facilitating Difficult Dialogues on Race* by Derald Wing Sue (2016)
- *The Role of Equity and Diversity in Early Childhood Education* by Krischa Esquivel and colleagues (2020)
- *Stamped: Racism, Antiracism, and You* by Jason Reynolds and Ibram X. Kendi (2020)
- *The Sum of Us: What Racism Costs Everyone and How We Can Prosper Together* by Heather McGhee (2021)
- *Why Are All the Black Kids Sitting Together in the Cafeteria? Conversations About Race* by Beverly Daniel Tatum (2017)

Much of the work we conducted around antiracism and antibias practices proved popular among humanities teachers. One district we worked with requested equity recommendations specifically for their math and science educators. To help that district, Vickie Lake and her colleagues at the University of Oklahoma recommended the following titles for science, technology, engineering, and math (STEM) teachers:

- *Braiding Sweetgrass: Indigenous Wisdom, Scientific Knowledge, and the Teachings of Plants* by Robin Wall Kimmerer (2020)

- *The Disordered Cosmos: A Journey into Dark Matter, Space-time, and Dreams Deferred* by Chanda Prescod-Weinstein (2021)
- *Equity in Science: Representation, Culture, and the Dynamics of Change in Graduate Education* by Julie R. Posselt (2020)
- *Indigenous Sustainable Wisdom: First-Nation Know-How for Global Flourishing* by Darcia Narvaez (Ed.) and colleagues (2019)
- *Mathematics for Equity: A Framework for Successful Practice* by Na'ilah Suad Nasir (Ed.) and colleagues (2014)
- *The Myth of Race: The Troubling Persistence of an Unscientific Idea* by Robert W. Sussman (2014)

If reading an entire book proves too time-consuming for the teacher, consider parsing out relevant chapters to read and discuss. For example, "Climbing Out of the Gap," Chapter 1 of *Culturally Responsive Teaching and the Brain* (Hammond, 2015), deals with assumptions about academic prowess and how teachers offer students practices to become, or not become, independent learners.

2.19: Use Classroom Data

Analyze classroom data for patterns of inequities. For example, consider which students, in terms of race, ethnicity, sex, or other factors, are doing what in these categories:

- **Student talk:** Who is talking and responding to questions?
- **Student participation:** Who is writing, speaking, or completing the learning tasks?
- **Attention:** How does the teacher encourage disengaged students to participate? Who gets more smiles, eye contact, proximity, and extended feedback and responses?
- **Tone of voice:** Who receives threats, sarcasm, and negative redirections? Who receives demanding expectations and positive intent?

- **Leadership:** Who sets academic and behavioral goals? Who has responsibilities or jobs in the class? Who leads the most in labs and athletic groups?
- **Visual confirmation:** Do students see scientists, authors, artists, mathematicians, and others who look like them in the classroom and in curriculum materials beyond the requisite Marie Curie of science and traditional holiday exposures?

2.20: Promote an Identity Growth Mindset

Stone and Heen (2014) point out the inevitability of clashes with other people's identities when providing coaching feedback. When coaching for equity, you may confront some basic philosophies or beliefs—ideas central to that person's identity. "I can't be racist; I'm a Christian" or "I'm not prejudiced; I'm the wife of a Mexican American" are comments we've heard from people who, at the same time, tout biased positions regarding students. In these instances, the teacher may reject the feedback because it attacks their identity, their sense of who they are.

Be prepared to talk candidly about identity when this happens. Identity is not forged in iron, regardless of how important that identity may be. This is what Stone and Heen (2014) mean by a *growth identity mindset*. Let the teacher know that identity changes. Maybe you were once a nervous and socially awkward teenager; now, as an adult, you may no longer be those things. The teacher may perceive coaching questions about the foundations of their identity as an attack on who they are. Assure the teacher this is not the case, and discuss the possibility of trying a growth identity mindset to view identity as evolving. Suggest the teacher consider this: "This is who I am right now; it might not be who I am in the future." Figure 2.2 shows how one educator drew her identity aspects. Her role as superintendent, an important identity for her two years earlier, shrunk when she retired, whereas her role as grandmother grew.

Figure 2.2   The Multiple Aspects of Identity

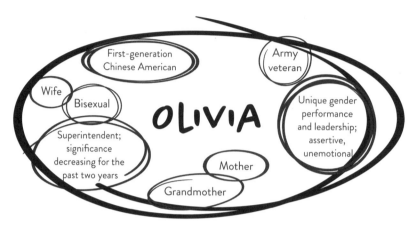

Another issue around identity occurs when a teacher overidentifies with only one aspect of their identity. This "all and nothing more" identity often occurs in adolescence, but it can sometimes happen with adults. For example, a teacher might hinge their entire identity on their role as a mother when, in reality, that is only one aspect of who they are. When you see this, help the teacher see all their significant identities. They may be mothers and still be educators, community members, veterans, sisters, runners, and so on—and the significance of one component of identity may shift over time.

2.21: Ensure Equitable Classroom Management

As early as preschool, some teachers overdiscipline some students and even target students of specific races and sexes (U.S. Department of Education Office for Civil Rights, 2014). This work is often unconscious; it's a blind spot for the teacher. Collect data about overusing a student's name in those instances or continually highlighting the misbehaviors of specific student populations. (The implementation story "Hakim's Not Here" illustrates this teacher behavior.) Give the teacher data and let them know that, unfortunately, this is not an uncommon issue. The most crucial point is changing a teacher's behavior and getting them to switch strategies to teach prosocial skills instead of always highlighting a student's negative aspects.

2.22: Relabel Language Learners

Encourage teachers to view students who are learning English as a second language as typical, as desired, and as an asset. As education consultant Angela Di Michele Lalor (2020) put it, "When teachers begin to look at what students understand, know, and can do, it changes the way the teacher and their students approach learning" (para. 15). Many countries work hard to produce multilingual students; the students themselves benefit, and they benefit this nation as highly communicative members of society, regardless of their current performance level on standardized assessments. It's an honor to teach them. In addition, dual-language learners use more of their brains than monolingual speakers, and their brain function is improved at all stages of life—from childhood to old age (DeLuca & Voits, 2022; Kliesch et al., 2022; Voits et al., 2020, 2022).

2.23: Use Department or Course Data

Review these data with the teacher and identify patterns of inequities. Use these questions as a guide:

- Who is successful in which courses?
- Who is recognized the most?
- Who missed the greatest number of days?
- Who is not enrolling in the course?
- Can honors students learn in classes with nonhonors students?

- Are some groups of students sent to the office more frequently than others?
- Do teachers provide frequent assessments of understanding, or are grades based on one comprehensive exam?
- Is it possible to move from points-based to standards-based grading?
- Are courses in social justice or advocacy offered?
- Regarding advanced placement and International Baccalaureate data, are there trends in demographics regarding passing, as opposed to enrolling in, the courses?

2.24: Review the Curriculum for Bias and Racism

Help the teacher review their curriculum for inequities. Identify and address the following issues:

- Include proper names and photos in assessment items that reflect student ethnicities and races.
- Offer mathematics, science, and physics problems in contexts that most students experience.
- Find opportunities to highlight positive current events from the students' heritage nations. Are contributions from ancient Arabic, Mayan, Chinese, and other cultures presented in the curriculum? Does the curriculum celebrate U.S. immigrant scientists?
- Ensure that students see in both the classroom and curriculum materials scientists, authors, chefs, mathematicians, performing artists, and others who look like them.
- Find ways to present men and women in nontraditional gendered work, such as pilots Bessie Coleman and Jackie Cochran.
- Let students know whose perspective dominates primary source documents. Is it that of the oppressed or the oppressor?

- How many of the textbooks and novels used in the curriculum have been written by women and people of color?
- Does the curriculum supplement the erased histories of Native Americans, Asian Americans, Mexican Americans, and LGBTQ+ Americans? Do students know how these communities contributed to the economic and social fabric of the United States?
- Does the curriculum present marginalized groups only in terms of their oppression? That is, there's more to being Black than slavery and more to being Jewish than the Holocaust. Find examples showing people's full humanity. Go beyond heroes and holidays when teaching about others. Review the books from author James Loewen about erased and erroneous information in curriculum and texts (such as *Lies My Teacher Told Me: Everything Your American History Textbook Got Wrong*). Do students know about Black Wall Street in Tulsa, tales of resilience from women and the LGBTQ+ community, the unfiltered history of the Alamo, and Black slaves' significant cultural influences on the United States?

Even if all students in the class are of one race or ethnicity, they benefit from encountering materials, scholars, leaders, and assessment items reflecting a diverse population. This practice enriches their lives and empowers them to work and live with various people in the future.

2.25: Interrupt Harmful Speech

Teach the teacher to speak up when they hear colleagues, students, or parents express stereotypes or dehumanizing comments. Offer these and other tactics for speaking out:

- If you're nervous, wait and practice with friends. Before you confront the person, check your intentions—that is, how you wish to come across in the meeting.
- You can always delay and revisit the conversation later with "Hey, I wanted to talk to you about something you commented on the other day. Here's what I wish I had mentioned." You don't always have to know the perfect response at the ideal time.
- Don't expect immediate change. Sometimes people think about something for a long time before they have a change of heart. But don't be complicit with your silence either.
- Try these questions and comments to flesh out motivations behind a belief or position: "Tell me more about this belief; how did you come to this understanding?" "I'm wondering if you've ever questioned this basic assumption."
- When you hear inappropriate language, offer alternative language you're learning. For example, simply comment, "Here's something you might say instead" or "I just learned this, and it made so much sense." If asked why, be ready to explain.
- When you hear an inappropriate joke, just keep repeating, "I don't get it." Often, when people have to explain, humor loses its power. Or be direct: "That's not cool or funny, and here's why."

2.26: Be Sensitive to Cultural Differences

Review your coaching in terms of cultural sensitivity. Likewise, help the teacher do the same with their classroom instruction and guidance. The Global Leadership and Organizational Behavior Effectiveness (GLOBE) work provides the most extensive study of cultural differences in approaches to leadership from more than 500 researchers in over 160 countries, contributing large-scale studies of culture, leadership, and trust. GLOBE defined *leadership* as an individual's ability to motivate and influence people to contribute successfully to an organization (Chhokar et al., 2019; House et al., 2014), an essential aspect of the coaching role.

The researchers identified nine components of culture, such as assertiveness, gender equality, and power distribution; these are worth checking out on their website at www.globeproject.com. Although cultural dimensions play out differently in various cultures, GLOBE revealed a few cross-cultural attributes (Chhokar et al., 2019; House et al., 2014). For example, almost all cultures prefer "participative leadership" and "employee involvement in decision making" over autocratic leadership. See Figure 2.3 for all nine components of the GLOBE dimensions.

Help the teacher review any classroom patterns noted using the dimensions. Are they favoring male or female contributions in the classroom? Are they valuing fairness, altruism, and kindness in the classroom? Do they promote a future-planning orientation with students? As you can see in Figure 2.3, there are universally desirable cultural dimensions that most cultures prefer (Chhokar et al., 2019; House et al., 2014). For example, multiple cultures valued excellence, high standards, innovation, and equitable power. By contrast, "power distributed unequally" was deemed less desirable. Numerous times throughout this book, we advocate involving the teacher in the decision-making process of coaching, pressing for excellence, and building trust; these practices provide a great deal of mileage in terms of driving cultural sensitivity into the coaching practice.

2.27: Listen for Generalizations

Words or phrases such as *all my students, these kids, everyone, never,* and *always* are abstractions. We often hear statements such as "These kids don't have the experiences they need to understand complex literature, so I use more simple texts." When you hear vague terms like *these kids* or *experiences,* press for specificity. Ask the teacher who used the terminology exactly how many students were involved or when the situation happened. Helping the teacher be more precise in their analysis and thinking helps them pick apart broader generalizations like racism and sexism.

Figure 2.3 GLOBE'S Nine Cross-Cultural Attributes

FUTURE ORIENTATION

is the value of gratification delay and future planning. Canada and Switzerland rank high in future orientation, while Russia and Argentina rank low.

PERFORMANCE ORIENTATION

is the degree to which innovation, standards, and exceptional performance are valued. Here, the U.S. and Europe rank high, while Greece and Russia rank low.

UNCERTAINTY AVOIDANCE

is about how comfortable people are with risk, change, and ambiguity. Japan avoids uncertainty, while the U.S. and India do not.

HUMANE ORIENTATION

is the degree to which fairness, altruism, and kindness are valued. Ireland and Egypt value a humane orientation, while France and Singapore tend not to.

ASSERTIVENESS

is the degree to which individuals use force and confrontation. The U.S. and Germany rank high in assertiveness. New Zealand and Switzerland rank low.

POWER DISTANCE

is the extent to which people accept an unequal distribution of power. India and Mexico accept power distance; the U.S. and Israel do not.

INSTITUTIONAL COLLECTIVISM

is the degree to which individuals distribute resources and take collective action. Japan and Singapore maintain strong institutional collectivism, and Italy and Germany do not.

IN-GROUP COLLECTIVISM

is the degree to which individuals value loyalty and cohesion to groups and families. China and India have high in-group collectivism. Finland and Sweden do not.

GENDER EQUALITY

is the degree to which female and male equality is valued. Sweden and Costa Rica value gender equity; Italy and Egypt, not so much.

2.28: Engage in Values Affirmation

Many classroom interventions focus on student deficits, whereas values affirmation focuses on student strengths. Have students respond to brief writing prompts about their most important personal issues—friends, family, and interests—at the start of the school year, before important tests, and around holidays. By writing about what they value, students relieve stress and improve academic and other outcomes.

This simple intervention of affirming personal values reduced the racial achievement gap by nearly 30 percent among beginning university students, and it had a more significant effect on students of color when compared to white students (Walton & Cohen, 2011). Moreover, a follow-up study conducted 10 years later with some of the same university students showed sustained positive effects for the students of color following university (Brady et al., 2020). Values affirmation activities were found to produce similar results in adolescents (Cohen et al., 2006; Goyer, 2017).

2.29: Build Collective Efficacy

As you observe a grade level or content area for equitable practices, coach the team using their collective data. For example, "In 3rd grade, during the lesson on main idea, 65 percent of the students participated in academic conversations. Of the 35 percent who did not, 20 percent are in special education, and 11 percent are dual-language learners. Let's work together today to develop strategies to engage those learners." This approach may surface the teachers' negative mental models about the students identified; if so, it becomes ever more crucial to focus on what the students *can* do. Working with this larger group enables individual teachers to grow as they learn that not all their colleagues see students the same way as they do. Coaches can use group coaching to change specific teachers' notions about how students learn.

2.30: Give Students Time to Rehearse

Often, teachers ask students to respond without allowing them to rehearse what they want to say. This procedure results in the extroverts and language-savvy students doing the most talking. Because people learn when they talk, all students need to speak. If students receive a chance to practice before addressing a large group, they are more likely to speak and are more likely to have thoughtful responses. What would this look like in a classroom?

2.31: Review Teacher Expectations of Students

Our work in classrooms with high-needs populations led to a frequent finding: some long-time educators of low-performing students may decrease their expectations for students. As a coach, if this is your target group of teachers or administrators, check that their expectations derive from typically performing students—not just the students they see year to year. Use student work examples, visits to other programs, videos, and other approaches to ensure they maintain solid, realistic expectations for their students. For example, you might ask a teacher who has remained in a self-contained special education class for years to come into a regular classroom of the same-age students to conduct a self-check of their academic presuppositions.

2.32: Acknowledge Student Cultures

Teachers must be aware of their own culture and the culture of the students in their classrooms. Students are looking for themselves in their learning space; they're asking, "How am I represented here?" Ask the teacher to list all the students in their classroom. Next to the student names, ask them to write one thing they know about that student and one thing they know about the student's cultural identity or background. If they have nothing personal to recall, it's their job to get to know the student and the student's family. Use this list with the strategies *use classroom data* and *review the curriculum for bias and racism.* Teachers who value students' identity and acknowledge cultural differences help students to see themselves in the world.

2.33: Encourage Student Debate

Encourage teachers to promote student disagreement with textbook content and other curriculum materials. Often, subjects are taught from the dominant culture's point of view without inclusive perspectives from multiple ethnicities or those without power. Reward students for questioning current and historical events that are unjust or problematic—events they may experience daily. Teachers can use topical events to discuss student culture, identity, or language and their representation (or lack thereof) in the curriculum.

2.34: Ask Reflective Questions

When coaching for equity, consider asking the following reflective questions:

- What generalizations might you be making here?
- What kind of data or research do you have to make this claim?
- Tell me more about your idea or belief. Maybe I could agree with you if I understood it better.
- Are there any ways you might be disempowering your students?
- What would an opponent of your approach say about it?
- What are the pros and cons of going in this direction?
- When you say _____, what belief or philosophy are you operating from? Is that belief serving you well? Is it serving your students?

- How did you come to this understanding?
- I'm wondering if you've ever questioned this basic assumption.

What It Looks Like in Practice

Look Who's Talking

Focus Strategies:
- Ask reflective questions
- Use classroom data
- Observe student academic thinking

While observing with a group of high school administrators and coaches eager to learn new strategies, Angela made the most of a learning opportunity regarding equity. She deployed the following strategies: *ask reflective questions, use classroom data,* and *observe student academic thinking.* The faculty studied engagement strategies, and one teacher was particularly excited to try a new student engagement technique and receive feedback. The teacher invited the administrators in to watch. The room setup included inside and outside circles, and students completed the prereading work necessary to prepare for discussion. During the observation, Angela noted that most of the students were students of color but that 90 percent of the speaking came from two white students. A few students of color offered snippets of information, and others acted as note takers and support for the speakers.

Following the observation, administrators were thrilled with students' high-level thinking in their remarks and use of this strategy. Angela let them talk for a couple of minutes and then asked three of them to go back to the classroom and come back and describe the students who had made significant verbal contributions to the seminar. The two came back a bit stricken; they were clear in their descriptions of the two white students and *one* student of color. The rest of the class never spoke substantially during the entire discussion. The rest of the observing group were dumbfounded that they had not noticed the inequity. They had an excellent talk about what their expectations were for the different populations of students and why. Change happened.

"Hakim's Not Here"

Focus Strategies:
- Ensure equitable classroom management
- Use classroom data

A coach Tamarra worked with recounted how a primary teacher they coached in Oakland, California, used the strategies *ensure equitable classroom management* and *use classroom data* to reflect on a situation that troubled her with a student named Hakim. The teacher repeatedly used his name to redirect him: "Hakim, get on the carpet." "Hakim, keep your hands to yourself." "Hakim, stop writing on your friend's paper." Habitually. Many teachers do this and forgo other, more appropriate strategies, particularly in early childhood classes. The negative redirect using the name can easily cause negative associations with the student.

In this case, the negative expectation sprung up elsewhere. One day Hakim was absent, and the teacher asked the class, "Who picked up my scissors? Who did that?" A student blurted, "It was Hakim!" Then the rest of the group responded in unison, "But Hakim's not here!" The teacher stood dumbfounded and humbled, realizing that they, as the teacher, were responsible for that low expectation among the students. The teacher vowed to no longer use names to redirect students and to remember the power of labeling a student in a community from that day forward. When it's in our control, we need to protect our students' reputations.

The Coach's Arm (Nearly) Falls Off

 Focus Strategies:

- Engage in difficult conversations
- Use social data
- Use signal coaching (see Chapter 8)

Tamarra worked with a coach in the Mission District of San Francisco who had a hard time helping a teacher manage a student in a special education classroom. The coach had asked the teacher to describe the positive aspects of the student. The teacher replied, "There are none. That's why I'm talking to you." Realizing the seriousness of the situation, Tamarra suggested the coach prepare her coaching session in writing. They worked together to write an outline that included the teacher's beliefs (this child was inherently bad); why the teacher had this belief; how this belief conflicted with the school's belief about children in general; and what practices could change the belief.

To help the teacher realize that this issue could have a positive resolution, the coach recounted a story about a similar student and a teacher who had successfully changed the child's school experience. She also explained a practice that might help the teacher see the student's positive traits. "I'll come to observe the student, and I'll sit not far from them," explained the coach. "Then every time I see the student meet any of your expectations, I'll wave my clipboard over my head. That's your signal to praise or describe what the student is doing. This way, we can get a bit of positive feedback to build off of." Reluctantly, the teacher agreed.

On the day of the in-class signal coaching, Tamarra was in the classroom observing the coach for training purposes. Within five minutes of the start of class, the coach's clipboard went up, and it came down only twice for a few seconds during the entire 50-minute lesson; the coach complained that her arm "nearly fell off." Afterward, in the coaching session, the teacher reflected on the data and explained how invisible the student's cooperation had been to her before the coach made it painfully clear. The teacher planned to get to know the student better and to notice their efforts to engage in the class. The coach displayed a powerful use of signal coaching, a format we look at in Chapter 8. Often, a coach's critical, in-class feedback helps a teacher reset expectations and engage in more equitable practices with students.

"*This* Is Expected of 11th Graders?!"

 Focus Strategy:
- Review general expectations

Keith and Angela coached for a few years in a handful of secondary schools in a large district that worked to integrate special education students and teachers into the regular education classes. This involved coaching, training, and planning at every level with every position in the school. The work was successful as measured by multiple factors, including surveys, interviews, and student achievement scores.

In particular, the special education teachers consistently stated that they had raised their academic expectations for their special needs students. These veteran teachers were accustomed to teaching students with considerable deficits in academic skills, and they felt with good reason that they were pros at supporting student improvement each year. However, when they joined a regular classroom teacher to coteach, they were stunned at what regular education students produced. One teacher remarked, "I always knew my learning standards for English language arts and asked students to identify the theme as they moved through a novel. I had no idea that 11th graders were more precisely expected to 'determine two or more themes or central ideas of a text and analyze their development over the course of the text including how they interact and build on one another to produce a complex account.'" As a result of participating in coteaching, they and several other wise special education teachers eagerly increased their expectations for their students as they gained a more nuanced understanding of what typical students were required to produce.

Confronting an Advanced Placement (AP) Teacher

Focus Strategies:

- Use classroom data
- Use department or course data
- Engage in difficult conversations

A high school coach in suburban Chicago told Keith about a difficult coaching conversation that took place with an AP English teacher. The teacher had posted in the syllabus and online course entry the following requirements: "This is an advanced course, and students must know how to conduct literary analysis before entering this course. Students without appropriate literary analysis skills will not be able to complete the course requirements." The coach planned a crucial, one-on-one conversation with the teacher to explain the consequences of such an approach on potential students.

During the conversation, the teacher defended the syllabus, saying, "I have high standards, and I'm tired of students not knowing how to analyze literature after 10 years of school. I'm not dumbing down my expectations." The coach acknowledged the concern and even empathized with the teacher about lowering expectations, having been a chemistry teacher for 12 years who had grown weary of reteaching mathematics that students should already have known. As the coach noted to the teacher, "I was frustrated because I wasn't even the math teacher; I was their science teacher. So I fully understand your issue. I've been in the same place."

However, the coach explained that an effort was in place to recruit students of color to take AP courses and that students reported they were afraid of this AP English teacher because "we're expected to know stuff we don't know." The coach went even further with another data point: "Besides, your state standards for English detail that students *will conduct literary analysis in this course by citing, determining, analyzing,* and so on—these are the goals of the course. The standards don't state that students must already know how to do all these things *before* the course begins." The coach argued that the teacher was putting in a prerequisite that shouldn't exist—and that by doing so, students who might potentially succeed in the class were being shut out. Reluctantly, the teacher agreed to the change.

Afterward, the coach and school counselor set up peer tutors for the students they drafted into the course. As they monitored the students for the next couple of years, they noted no issues, with their target students successfully scoring 4s and 5s on the AP exams and successfully completing the challenging course.

Several actions paved the way for this successful resolution of a difficult conversation:

- The coach did their homework reviewing the learning standards, gathering student data, and using data from the teacher's syllabus.
- The coach prepped the following points crucial to having successful difficult conversations:
  » They wrote out counterarguments for claims they anticipated from the AP teacher.
  » They jotted down their intent behind the situation, who they wanted to *show up as* in the conversation. They wrote, "I'm a passionate and calm student advocate."
  » They thought about how they might empathize with or acknowledge some of the teacher's concerns.
  » They took the time to do a dress rehearsal of the conversation with a trusted friendly critic—the counselor—beforehand.

In the end, the coach confronted a gatekeeper, broke a tiny systemic barrier, and opened a door of opportunity nonexistent to students before.

Coaches, Consider This...

- What challenge do you encounter when it comes to coaching equity?
- List a few out-of-the-box strategies you'll add to your repertoire of coaching skills.
- What pieces of social data do you have or can you collect regarding the power of high academic and social expectations for students of color?

3

Coaching Academic Instruction

This chapter is all about building the teacher's instructional repertoire and helping them make thoughtful choices about what to incorporate in lessons; it's about coaching academic instruction. The teacher's skill at delivering high-quality academic instruction is crucial to productive teaching (Costa et al., 2016), and coaching academic instruction is the coach's most typical job. Hattie (2012) showed that strong educators prove exceptionally gifted in this area. They establish a stable environment for learning, continually check understanding and student input, and are proficient at finding ways to represent content for students. Moreover, Kim and colleagues (2019) found that high-performing instructors valued high achievement in themselves and others.

Following are a wide range of moves that help teachers gain a passion for the technical aspects of teaching and learning.

Researcher	Effective Teacher Traits or Dispositions Related to Academic Instruction
Costa et al. (2016)	• Skillfulness: desires to be professionally explicit, elegant, precise
Hattie (2012)	• Identifies the most important ways to represent the content • Monitors learning and provides feedback • Believes all students can reach the success criteria
Kim et al. (2019)	• Conscientiousness: ambitious, highly responsible, organized

Strategies

3.1: Start Small

Target one primary academic goal. Include specific steps to ensure the teacher is successful. Focus on one aspect of the curriculum or one small group of students. Work on one course or one subject area with the teacher. Like a blocked writer staring at a blank screen, when a teacher is overwhelmed or stressed, they cannot move; they need to begin one small task.

3.2: Specify Language

To help the teacher think about specificity in instruction, make sure you both understand the language frequently tossed around in education. Ask, "How do you define _____?" or "Give me an example of what you mean by _____." Unfortunately, many educators make assumptions about what common terms like *mastery, learning, formative assessment, professional learning communities, care,* and so on mean. Often, coaches are surprised to learn that the teacher maintains a different understanding of a concept even though they both attended the same training, read the same book on the topic, or use the words almost daily. Formative assessment is often misunderstood. In one instance, teachers were instructed about formative assessment and even planned a writing assessment together, but when they brought student artifacts back, it became apparent that the implementation had been vastly different. One classroom had used templates, one had supplied a paragraph frame, and one had given the students no support for the formative assessment. In another example, two grade levels at the same school, after the same training, conducted professional learning community (PLC) meetings. One was the model of collaborative planning with all participants taking responsibility for meeting the needs of all learners. The other grade level looked at some student work and spent their time making a list of what students needed to master prior to their current grade level. The two grade levels maintained vastly different understandings of the term *PLC* following the same training.

3.3: Accept Adults' Reluctance to Admit Errors

Experienced adult learners may only reluctantly admit a lack of skills and may mask a lack of knowledge with a lack of will. That is, they may appear unmotivated when it comes to learning something new. Provide coaching without the expectation that the adult will respond, "I didn't know that." Give your advice, brainstorm, or lead reflection nonetheless, and don't always assume the teacher will automatically know all the fundamentals you might expect. To broaden your background in adult learning theory, review Knowles et al.'s work (2020) and look ahead to adult learner characteristics in Chapter 7. Determine if you're addressing those needs in coaching.

3.4: Focus on Data

Instead of providing coaching feedback based on your opinion, use data to support your praise or critical claims. Consider a variety of data points:

- Student work samples
- Student interviews
- Course enrollment or completion data
- Assessment results from curriculum materials, district formative assessments, and state or national tests
- Environment rating scales
- Parent surveys
- Observation checklists of students or teachers
- Photos or videos
- Classroom artifacts
- Individualized student education plans
- Textbook or teacher-made questions and assignments
- Curriculum implementation checklists
- Software usage reports
- Scripts of teacher or student performance
- Lesson plans

Even when you're coaching soft skills or dispositions that seem harder to capture—such as tone of voice, warmth, enthusiasm, care, sarcasm, or joy—if you look carefully enough, you'll find data points that communicate the concept. Is the teacher sighing and rolling their eyes before responding to the student? Are they telling students they will love this new topic and explaining *why* they'll be so enthusiastic about it? Is the teacher lowering or raising their voice or smiling at this point? Is the preschool teacher on their knees at eye level with students or standing across the room trying to redirect them? Find the tiny data points needed for coaching, even the most elusive characteristics. Always coach from data.

3.5: Do This Every Day, All the Time

Sometimes new skills are hard to stick to. For example, a teacher may produce a strategy once in front of you and then not show it again. To promote full implementation from teachers, try phrases such as these:

- "You need to do this at every available opportunity."
- "Do this at the next available opportunity."
- "Students need to encounter this action every single day in every class."
- "You need to produce this when I'm not present and for the remainder of your career."
- "Regardless of the focus of the district, school, or state, this is a best practice for all time."

Tell teachers to implement the practice when you're not around, when only students are present—that is, *all the time*. Be clear that this work is to become a part of their regular professional practice.

3.6: Provide Corrective Feedback

Be confident in providing critical constructive feedback to adults: "The correct label for that action is _____." "Let's try this again." "No, that's not what we planned." "Tell me why that's not an example of _____." "You had the first part right. Here's how to complete the strategy." Adults are not fragile, and most can make a mistake without being devastated by it (Harmin & Toth, 2006; Saphier et al., 2018); they're not powerless toddlers or soft egg yolks. To this point, multiple researchers highlight the significance of both positive and frank, critical feedback (e.g., Anderson, 2014; Fishbach & Finkelstein, 2020; Fishbach et al., 2010; Fong et al., 2018; Hargrove, 2008; Killion, 2019; Zenger & Folkman, 2014). Be kindhearted, use precise data, be humble, describe how to correct the issue, and provide explicit critique—all at the same time; these combined attributes are not mutually exclusive.

3.7: Hang Out

Pick up your papers, notebook, or computer, and sit in a teacher's classroom for long periods of time. You might take notes and provide in-class coaching. Other times, you could work with a student one-on-one or analyze the teacher's coaching notes and plan the upcoming coaching conversation. Simply increasing your presence in the room may improve the teacher's practice and remind them to implement their commitments.

3.8: Whisper Feedback

Think about gently nudging the teacher during teaching with a whisper to implement the practices planned or provide a handwritten note or quick instructions on a small whiteboard. Sometimes, all a teacher needs is a nudge during teaching to fully implement a practice. For this and other structures, see the 18 coaching formats listed in Chapter 8.

3.9: Observe Another Teacher

Take the struggling teacher to see an outstanding teacher. Be sure you accompany the teacher. You want to make sure they see what you see. Sometimes they look at something you don't intend for them to notice and take away less meaningful practices. For example, we've seen teachers focus on the number of special needs students in the room or the size of the classroom library when in actuality, their job was to detail curriculum practices. Avoid this error by providing personal guidance concerning what specific practice they should look for during the observation and ensuring the time is used purposefully. Prior to the observation, decide what is to be observed—perhaps which students do and do not participate in academic conversations or how the teacher redirects those who do not.

3.10: Use Models of Teaching and the Principles of Learning

Both new and experienced teachers gain proficiency by labeling and intentionally using specific models of teaching and the 24 principles of learning—and coaches must be knowledgeable of these practices. Some teachers use the models or principles by coincidence, whereas others use them intentionally. Either way, even a cursory knowledge of these designs makes for a more powerful coach.

Models of teaching (more recently referred to as *models of student learning*) are the broader categories of instruction and curriculum that teachers use to set up their learning environment, goals, questions, and activities; these models exist in specific philosophies or theories. There are four families of models, an easy set of information for the coach to acquire (Joyce et al., 2017).

The *social models* involve group problem solving and responsibility and include models such as cooperative learning, group investigations, and role-play. The *behavioral models* address basic facts, skills, and concepts and are composed of models such as mastery learning, direct instruction, and simulations. The *information-processing models* are more about generalizations, thinking skills, and principles and include models such as concept attainment, inductive thinking, and inquiry. Finally, the *personal teaching models* are about individual problem solving and creativity; they include models such as nondirective teaching, formats for classroom meetings, and synectics (an approach to problem solving that focuses on cultivating creative thinking).

Concerning the principles of learning, you'll find the best summary of them in Chapter 12 of *The Skillful Teacher* (Saphier et al.,

2018). The principles of learning help teachers identify the significance of moving from concrete to abstract representations, avoiding close confusers, using modeling, engaging students, and so on—the most common tactics for increasing students' rate and retention of learning. Combine this knowledge with the work of Hattie and Fisher (Fisher et al., 2016, 2017; Hattie, 2022), and you'll possess many basic tenets of curriculum and instruction.

3.11: Clarify Your Role as Coach

Be clear about what your job is; explain it. If the teacher remarks that you're hypercritical or that you seem to be calling them a failure, consider the following responses: "I think your work is commendable with the skills and tools you have; it's my firm belief that everyone has room to improve." "I give feedback even to the highest performers; that's the job of a coach." "It's not my job to be hypercritical. It's my job to provide you with areas of strengths and weaknesses." If you know something about the teacher's interests and can make a connection, remind them of activities where they received feedback. Tell them that even the most famous people we know have a coach. Ask the teacher, "Where would _____ (a famous athlete, leader, or musician) be without _____ (name their coach)?"

3.12: Try Triple-Column Lesson Design

To move a practice into a habit, try this approach, which requires the teacher to use three columns for planning. The first column lists the actions the teacher takes throughout the lesson, such as stating the lesson objective and rationale. In the second column, the teacher lists what the students do, which corresponds to the action listed in the first column. The third column indicates the precise steps the teacher needs to take for students to implement the targeted skill, such as arranging for small-group work, teaching concept development, or differentiating instruction for dual-language learners or special needs students. For an example of what this looks like, take a peek at Chapter 6.

3.13: Use Social Data (Stories)

Consider a story as social data. Relate an account of an excellent teacher who changed after coaching and increased academic outcomes. Sometimes a well-placed narrative illustration communicates better than a research reference.

3.14: Encourage Guided Teacher Reading

Provide readings on academic instructional strategies, and let the teacher respond to the task rather than to you. For example, you might say the following:

> As you read, use a yellow highlighter to mark what you know, do, and feel comfortable with. Use a pink highlighter for what makes you wonder, what makes you curious, or what you would like to try. Use an orange highlighter for something that might not fit with your teaching style.

Coach using the yellow ideas (prior knowledge) to encourage the pink highlighted ones (current interests). Decide on a pink notation they will try, such as having students rehearse saying their ideas out loud before sharing with the whole class. Be ready to debrief. The orange notes (what doesn't fit their teaching style) help you build a relationship with the teacher as you learn about their preferences. This simple text coding helps teachers structure their thoughts as they reflect on the reading.

3.15: Use a Balanced Approach

Consider using both inquiry (asking lots of open-ended questions) and advocacy (clearly stating your opinion as a coach). Use a situational approach. Teachers who are new to the profession, new to this subject or age group, or stressed may not have the mental or emotional access to countless strategies; you (and they) may need to rely more on your expertise. On the other hand, if the teacher is highly skilled and reflective, your best match is most likely solid inquiry. This switching of approaches between inquiry and advocacy demonstrates a practical application of situational leadership theory (Northouse, 2022).

3.16: Ask Simple Questions

Ask, "Who learned what in the lesson today?" or "Who demonstrated what independently?" These straightforward questions get to the heart of what is happening in the classroom. With these questions, you lead the teacher in examining multiple aspects of the lesson. (Check out the implementation stories "Who Learned What?" and "Who Produced Thinking Independently?" at the end of this chapter to see this strategy in action.) Stay focused on the *who*, and make the teacher tell or show you data—student work, writing, artifacts, and so on—to defend their response. The process is cathartic, and the teacher often diagnoses the learning problems themselves using these simple, reflective prompts. Further, using an equity lens and asking, "Who learned what?" provides an opportunity to see whether the teacher intentionally engaged students of marginalized communities in the lesson.

3.17: Ensure Teachers Use Academic Language

Encourage the teacher to refrain from lapsing into kid-speak rather than modeling academic language. For example, students know the phrase *my bad,* and the teacher might use that slang, but students need to practice "Apologies for my error—let me correct it," which is the language the teacher needs to model. If the teacher tells you they use slang to build relationships and relate to the students, explain that, as the teacher, they may be the only role model the student has for academic speech or writing; there are multiple other approaches to building relationships with students. Requiring students to learn domain-specific and academic words provides one of the kindest, most generous gifts they can offer. Students want to know that teachers believe they can achieve challenging goals. An inspirational teacher communicates this belief, in large part, by the verbal model they provide.

3.18: Engage in ICU: Intensive Coach Use

Use intensive, one-on-one coplanning and observing for several weeks. We call this type of work ICU (intensive coach use). We recommend the coach combine it with task analysis and instructional planning multiple times a week, for eight rounds of intensive coaching over eight weeks, working on complete lessons or units of study. (For more details about ICU, see Chapter 6.)

In the beginning, the coach articulates and models the thought process with continual think-alouds. This first coaching session may be a two- or three-hour minitraining on task and data analysis concerning a learning standard or foundation. By session 4 or 5, the teacher takes the lead by articulating their thinking during planning. Finally, in the debrief, the coach shifts to more reflective conversations or questions. Observations after coplanning may involve the coach in whispering suggestions, signaling them in other ways, or coteaching in the classroom. WestEd (2016) calls this the POD process—plan, observe, debrief—an approach derived from microteaching, a researched process for teacher learning (Allen & Eve, 1968; Leong et al., 2021).

ICU work is meant to be short term. After a round or two of ICU cycles, the teacher returns to the regular coaching cycle. Unfortunately, most schools and coaches don't have the time or resources to continue this intensity of support over extended periods, such as over an entire school year or a semester. It's much like a medical ICU: people go there for short-term, intensive assistance and leave, ideally, in better shape.

3.19: Have the Teacher Write Out Steps

Have the teacher script out lessons or activities step-by-step, minute-by-minute (Lemov, 2021). Be specific about the steps, including "(1) Have students pick up whiteboards, pens, and eraser cloths as they enter. (2) Ask students to take their materials to their desks and take 90 seconds to respond to the question on the board on their whiteboards in five or fewer words. (3) Have students tap pens with their partners. (4) Instruct the partner with the longest hair to share their answer first." Some teachers respond, "This is *way* too much work. It's impossible to maintain for multiple lessons over time." Agree with this point and explain that this tactic is just for one set of lessons or a specific strategy and only for a short time. If the teacher agrees to this practice, after about six or eight times, they'll often become proficient and no longer need to maintain the detailed, didactic approach.

3.20: Articulate Your Thinking

As a coach, use think-alouds when modeling lesson plans for teachers. The think-aloud involves verbally articulating what you're thinking and why you're thinking it as you do something (Saphier et al., 2018). At a minimum, explain your rationale repeatedly. You're modeling for the teacher what's going on inside your head as you decide about instruction, planning, or data analysis. For example, as a coach, you might state aloud, "As I look at independent practice, I'm going to make sure I have an extension activity just in case one or two of my students got the concept early on. The last time I taught this, I was surprised that a few students needed enrichment, and I had no materials ready. I may not need this, but I want it as a backup." "Teacher thinking about a lesson" compared to the "teacher production of a lesson" is analogous to an iceberg (see Figure 3.1). The tip of the iceberg is the lesson with students, whereas the planning process is the bulk of the iceberg hidden underwater.

Figure 3.1   The Live Lesson–And the Thinking Behind It

THE LIVE LESSON
The Performance
On-Stage Production
In-Flight Operation
Intraoperative Surgery Phase

LESSON PREP: THE THINKING BEHIND THE LESSON
The Practice
Off-Stage Rehearsal
Flight Plan
Preoperative Surgery Phase

When you show or visit a powerful lesson, a struggling teacher may miss the tremendous amount of thought and planning that went into the design of that lesson—the part you don't see. When coaches use think-alouds, they help teachers bridge the gap between the final performance and the work that went into the preparation and rehearsal of a lesson.

3.21: Continually Make Connections

Repeatedly explain connections within the curriculum and instruction. Have the teacher explain the relationships aloud to you as well. How do these lessons align with the standards? How does this learning goal align with the student handout? How does this strategy link to students with special needs in the class? More often than not, the school's curriculum and standards were not designed with special needs students, Black students, or Latinx students in mind. Teachers must make these types of connections themselves. Find stories and examples that go beyond the typical cultural heroes that are inclusive of marginalized communities and multiple ethnicities and identities. Always think of the big picture and small steps.

Making connections is like planting a garden. Rather than haphazardly planting your vegetables, you consider the space each one needs, whether one plant will provide shade for another, whether you should set herbs apart because cultivating them is different, whether the roots of one will overwhelm the others, and so on. Just as in teaching, you must consider the connections among seemingly separate things and how those connections might change with time.

3.22: Promote the Use of Job Aids

Job aids provide small, portable procedural steps, to-do lists, or reminders of work requirements (Harless, 1986). Often visual, the job aid is anything from a checklist to a troubleshooting guide. Found in various industries (Willmore, 2018), the work reminders are an efficient follow-up to teacher training or coaching.

Figures 3.2 and 3.3 show job aids we've seen coaches use with teachers. As shown in Figure 3.2, the first sign hung at eye level beside the desk of school turnaround principal Sammie Cervantez of Bakersfield, California, and depicted four classroom doors, each with its door number. The principal's coach suggested this reminder so the principal wouldn't get caught too long at the computer during school hours. And it prompted Cervantez to get into the classrooms of the school's highest-need students.

Figure 3.2   Job Aid 1: A Reminder for the Principal

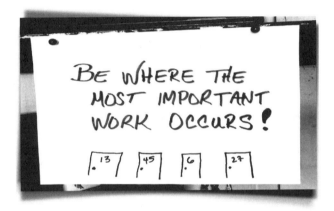

Coaches used the job aid shown in Figure 3.3 to help preschool teachers in the Los Angeles Unified School District ask students open-ended questions when interacting with books. Coaches asked teachers to write examples (on sticky notes) and nonexamples (on different-colored sticky notes) of open-ended questions. (The example here is from *Aveyan & Addyn's Very Good Day* [Almeida, 2020].) This job aid helped make the habit stick.

Other creative job aids coaches found successful with teachers included these:

- Annotate the teacher's lesson plan with suggestions, colored codes, or sticky notes that remind them of new habits.
- Place colorful signs, table tents, or sentence strips at eye level near where the teacher stands or sits.

- For habits that require regular intervals, ask the teacher to set multiple timers for audible cues to make transitions, ask questions, or engage in a new practice.
- Suggest more physical reminders for those teachers who may benefit from this approach, such as a note on a name badge hung around the neck, a label stuck to their sleeve, or a notation on a paper bracelet.
- For a more innovative approach, do what one coach witnessed a high school teacher do: the teacher assigned a student to remind them to review the lesson's success criteria and rationale. Basically, the adolescent was a living job aid.

Figure 3.3 Job Aid 2: Examples and Nonexamples of Open-Ended Questions

3.23: Offer Choices

Adults love choices (Knowles et al., 2020). Instead of telling the teacher how to solve a problem right away, ask them to brainstorm solutions. You can offer solutions as well. When you have a handful of ideas, ask the teacher to select the one they like best or the one that best matches their students' needs. If the teacher can't come up with any ideas, offer three or four for the teacher to choose among. Then set a time to come into the classroom and see the solution in action with students. Offer options concerning when and where to implement changes—for example, in the next class, the next week, or the next small or whole group. (See Chapter 7 for more about adult learners.)

3.24: Define Critical Thinking

Teachers have many misconceptions about the definition of *critical thinking*, particularly regarding the meanings of *analysis* and the individual words *creative* and *thinking*. Clarify the meaning and use an authoritative source. Instead of relying on popular and cute graphics that incorrectly label a researcher's concept, go straight to the original works. For K–12 work, we frequently recommend that coaches, principals, and instructional leadership teams dive directly into the works of Anderson and colleagues (2001) or Webb (2002, 2007, 2012). Then, with solid criteria for thinking in hand, the teacher can look for critical thinking evidence in the student's writing, speaking, or other work product and not solely in the teacher's lesson objective or activity description. What did students produce? How does that student work align with a specific level of thinking?

3.25: See the Problems That Students Are Solving

Minds tend to think critically when developing a solution to a problem; ask the teacher to tell you what problem students are solving. If students are not solving problems, ask what problem they might solve using new information. For example, if students are having a conversation about what started World War I and why it was significant, ask, "What problem might knowing this information solve?" Additionally, have teachers ask students, "What are you thinking?" rather than "What are you doing?"

3.26: Promote Student Leadership

Lead the teacher through an exercise that enables students to discuss the standard and their own learning needs. Post the standard, and let students work in pairs to develop what they think it means, using print and electronic resources. Some learners may need start-up guides or prompts; all should use a structured discussion strategy to explain the standard. Give feedback and add any missing points. Then let students work individually to brainstorm what they need to produce to show they know the standard. Have students set goals and write success criteria. Review the goals throughout the unit of study.

3.27: Provide More Frequent Feedback

Sometimes simply increasing the frequency of coaching conversations is enough to boost the teacher's use of strategies and practices the coach has targeted for improvement. Perhaps the teacher needs feedback multiple times a week. Don't be upset when a teacher fails to implement a given practice immediately following training. A few teachers simply need you to reteach the concept to them one-on-one. They're not trying to be difficult; they may simply not grasp an idea in a whole-group setting.

3.28: Stop Talking

If the teacher doesn't grasp the concept, revisit the issue in another way: role-play or draw the concept during a feedback conversation. Try a less chatty approach to the coaching, such as using a video example, visiting another program, providing a visual, or turning the coaching session into a make-and-take, where they construct something needed in the lesson.

A make-and-take might be the teacher leaving with an image of the mathematical computation for a real-life problem or creating a list of open-ended questions for higher-level thinking during a read-aloud. Constructing a takeaway during coaching may help the teacher implement the coaching suggestion, more than just talking about the issue.

3.29: Coteach with the Teacher

Take on half or even a tiny part of the lesson. Plan together, and let the teacher lead. Take on a small detail that the teacher struggles with, and model the practice live with their students. For example, the teacher may need help with redirection to engage all learners so they agree to coteach a lesson side-by-side. The teacher will deliver the information and ask the questions directing students to write answers on their whiteboards. When three students don't show their whiteboards, the coach takes over and says, "Ah, we have almost everyone. Let's take 15 seconds and let everyone finish, then I will ask you to show me your work row by row so I can see all your amazing work." Ask the teacher to take notes during your part. Debrief the lesson later. We describe this approach in greater detail in Chapter 8.

3.30: Ensure Full Production of a Practice

Don't address other issues with the teacher until the current practice you're targeting is consistently in place. After the teacher exhibits this new practice half a dozen times or so, move on to the next point. Continue to pay close attention to implementation; if the teacher regresses and stops the first practice while working on the second or third one, simply move coaching back to the first issue. Tell the teacher what is happening, and work toward full production of the first practice. Coaches often find that future work performance moves more rapidly if they go a bit slower at the beginning, working on the complete execution of a concept or skill. For more on this approach, which we call Target Coach, check out the 18 coaching formats listed in Chapter 8.

3.31: Realize That Lack of Evidence *Is* Evidence

Copiously scripting the teaching event is essential to addressing academic instruction. When teachers see and hear their own words or actions, it has a more significant effect on them than your "general impressions" about their work. In addition, when an absence of data in the script surfaces, use it to illustrate to the teacher the missed opportunities inherent in the observed lesson. Use that *lack of data* as evidence in the coaching conversation.

For example, when we coach teachers on active participation, we use a running record of precisely how many students are writing, speaking, or performing throughout the lesson. Then we contrast those numbers with the total number of students in the class, numerically displaying the positive and negative effects—who was engaged and who wasn't. Time and again, these data are eye-opening for the teacher.

Figure 3.4 shows how one coach used their script to coach from both data and lack of data; this graphic made a point with little need for more discussion. (The teacher's question to the students was "How does genetic variation among organisms in a species affect survival and reproduction?") Each *X* represents a student. The note "no idea" means that one student's paper was blank because they didn't have the background knowledge to answer the question. The dots represent students who mixed up the lesson vocabulary *effect* and *affect*. A dot with no slash marks means the student blurted out incomprehensible comments. An *X* with no dot *and* no slashes indicates the student didn't speak at all. The coach used these notes to coach from a "lack of evidence." There was no teacher scaffolding for correct vocabulary usage, a lack of student participation, and a failure of students to verbalize complete thoughts or sentences.

Figure 3.4   Coaching from Lack of Evidence

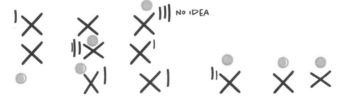

3.32: Include Others

Encourage the teacher to share successes and missteps with other teachers also implementing the new strategy. Do this in department meetings, professional learning communities, grade-level meetings, or staff development activities. (For gregarious teachers who like group collaboration, consider offering the strategy *set up a community of practice,* which we share in Chapter 7.)

3.33: Vlog

Show teachers before-and-after videos of their performance. Sometimes, viewing the new change is more potent for the teacher than hearing the coach describe the differences. This is why before-and-after weight-loss pictures are so dramatic. Alternatively, you can show the teacher the "before" video and draft questions the teacher can use to coach themselves going forward. These ideas are examples of both self-coach and video coach, as described in Chapter 8.

3.34: Create New Habits

Approximately half of our daily routines are habitual in our personal and work lives (Stanier, 2016; Wood et al., 2002). Help teachers create new patterns by experimenting with two variables—*context* and *specificity of action,* two significant determinants of success in building new habits (Klockner & Verplanken, 2019). For example, have the teacher try a new practice in a different context. Stand in a different place in the classroom to start the lesson—change the context—or have the teacher set a definite and more specific plan of action instead of a general one. As an example, instead of saying, "I'm going to try this," the teacher might say, "I am going to stop asking one student at a time to answer a question and use signaling to allow all students to answer." When people provide a brief plan for enactment, they're more likely to take action.

3.35: Identify Possibilities for Integration

Help the teacher find places to overlap content areas, and find ways for students to encounter integrated learning experiences. For example, does a center activity help the student practice both language and mathematics? Does a project promote complex mathematics and scientific skills? In a character analysis paper, does the teacher require students to use both fiction and nonfiction texts? How can the teacher include stories, research, people, and erased histories from communities of color in their curriculum? As a coach, you sometimes possess a broader perspective of the fully developed curriculum and see connections more quickly than a teacher. Bring your global perspective into the conversations when needed.

3.36: Ask Reflective Questions

Consider asking the teacher the following contemplative questions when coaching academic instruction:

- How are student outcomes changing compared with previous classes or groups?
- How are things going with the content or student learning?
- What's your biggest fear with this direction?
- What's the history behind this concept/subject area?
- What part of this unit or set of texts speaks to the lives of your students?
- Is there anything else? What more do you need?
- What's your challenge in this area?
- Whose perspective is missing from this unit, text, or historical event? Is a marginalized group neglected in the curriculum?
- What's your best hope with this group, line of questioning, lab experience, and so on?
- How can you get your students to this goal quicker or more efficiently?
- What are your students' literacy practices outside the classroom? What do they read and write? "How do they speak? In what ways do they know the world around them?" (Muhammad, 2020, p. 61)
- What misconceptions do you anticipate?

Notice that none of these are leading questions. They're not offering a suggestion masked as a question, such as "I'm wondering what would happen if you did _____?" "Have you ever tried _____?" "Did you think of _____?" "How might you _____?" If you have a direction or suggestion, just say it. If you really are asking a valid, open-ended question, ask it and *be prepared for any response* from the teacher. Be ready for them to go in a direction that opposes your opinion. If that happens, what is your plan to move forward from there in the dialogue? How will you address the conflicting views early in the conversation and keep the teacher receptive to feedback? For other ideas about starting and continuing a coaching conversation without relying on constrictive, open-ended questions, see Figure 8.1 (pp. 224–225).

3.37: Shadow a Student

Have the teacher observe a student in other learning environments and annotate how frequently the student writes or speaks academic vocabulary, writes in complete sentences and paragraphs, uses the schoolwide instructional focus, has their comments extended, responds to DOK 2 or 3 prompts, and so on. Debrief the results with the teacher after the observation to compare what the student encountered in various settings and what the teacher witnesses during their time with the student. Does the teacher possess insights into their instruction? Can the teacher provide ideas to help other educators who work with this student?

3.38: Differentiate Between Novice and Expert Teachers

Based on recommendations from the National Academies of Sciences, Engineering, and Medicine (NASEM, 2018), distinguish between how you approach new teachers as opposed to experienced teachers using the following suggestions:

- When problem solving with expert teachers, focus on the big picture, more significant concepts, or the rationale of the practice you're working on; experts frequently approach problems from this perspective.

- Focus on more procedural matters with the newbie. Novices tend to obsess over smaller, actionable details.
- Work with experts on conditionalized knowledge—the when, where, and why of using a specific skill or concept. For example, if a seasoned teacher is trying a new model of teaching, such as concept attainment, help them analyze which concepts in their standards might work best for the new model or philosophy. Point out details they might have missed and act as a sounding board. Another scenario may include a seasoned science teacher who is accustomed to developing all the experiments for their students and having students follow the directions to implement the investigation. New standards suggest students plan and develop investigations themselves. The teacher might therefore need help deciding which investigations they feel most comfortable handing over to students and which ones they might need to continue to guide more directly.
- Because novices frequently struggle to retrieve information, they take more time to think about problems and put actions into place. Therefore, you may need to coach them more regularly than more experienced teachers. Exercise patience when inexperienced teachers struggle with introductory practices.
- When working with virtuoso teachers, prepare your analysis of the problem at hand carefully. Experts will often question it. Be ready for them to debate your judgment when looking at the root causes of problems with student learning or with the delivery of a curriculum.
- Because novice teachers are working on the fluency of their practice, they may need many more repetitions of a method to master it. That's why we're big advocates of role-playing during a coaching session. The more the teacher practices with you or in a small-group setting, the more their fluency

and delivery of a method will improve and the greater the likelihood that they will quickly integrate the skill.

- In general, novice teachers prefer more praise and less critical feedback. By contrast, expert teachers value critical feedback more than praise. This is because praise tends to improve *work commitment,* whereas criticism is *more informative or instructional* (Fishbach & Finkelstein, 2020; Fishbach et al., 2010). Newer teachers may be less committed to the profession or job and may need more recognition to increase their commitment to work. By contrast, experienced teachers frequently possess more job security that doesn't need stabilizing; they want feedback to get them to the top of their game. We're not implying that you should only give praise to less experienced teachers and never praise pros; we're suggesting that skillful coaches shift the type and amount of feedback they offer according to the teacher's experience and context. Altering the type and frequency of praise means operating tenets of situational leadership theory (Northouse, 2022), one of the theoretical frameworks of this book.

3.39: Use Simple Illustrations

We do so much talking in coaching and education in general. We're *so* incredibly verbal that it's easy to forget some people are not high-verbals; they prefer moving in a role-play or seeing an illustration. Frequently, we take a T-chart or grid and stick information into it. Just that quick delineation of information adds clarity to a coaching point. Think of the concepts you coach about most frequently. How can you show that concept or skill in a super-simple graphic or illustration? Craft a drawing and try it out; it might help get your point across when you're working with a reluctant audience.

Mayer and Anderson (1991) found that when students studied with both pictures and words, they retained more information, which we found to be the case with teacher learners. Further, Fiorella and Mayer (2016) determined that students learned more when the instructor drew the graphic live during teaching instead of simply displaying the drawing.

Figures 3.5 and 3.6 show two of our favorite graphics that we created (or borrowed) over the years. Veteran educator Ian Guidera in Los Angeles uses the graphic shown in Figure 3.5 when coaching teachers on students' shouted-out random responses, called SOBO for short (shout-out, blurt-outs). The lines represent students. The tall lines with the circles represent the students who are blurting out. The teacher immediately sees that they're getting responses from only those few students who are the loudest or quickest in the class. The more equitable remedy would be to provide a system to hear *all* voices (Hattie & Clarke, 2019). The quick illustration often makes the point faster and better than merely talking.

Figure 3.5   Using Illustrations: Shout-Outs, Blurt-Outs (SOBO)

We often use the illustration shown in Figure 3.6 when discussing students' use of academic language. It drives home the point that students need to see, hear, speak, and write the lesson vocabulary regularly to retain it (Beck et al., 2013). Frequently, students only see and hear the words.

Figure 3.6   Using Illustrations: What It Takes to Learn Academic Vocabulary

3.40: Differentiate Between Big and Little Data

Big data involve district, state, and national testing, English-learner testing, district benchmarks, and schoolwide formative assessments—assessments the teacher did not design. Little data refer to the classroom or grade-level data collected in real time. These are typically designed and gathered by the teacher and include formative classroom assessments, anecdotal notes, and a lesson or unit assessment. Help the teacher compare and contrast how big data do and don't correlate with little data; sometimes there's alignment, and sometimes they don't reveal the same student needs. For example, sometimes classroom data (little data) show a high level of mastery of a given standard, but the standardized assessment (big data) does not. This could be a signal to the teacher that students are not retaining the information over time. Often, that may mean students need to do more independent thinking as they learn, complete an application of the skill or concept, or practice the skill more.

Another provocative approach to formative classroom assessment involves asking the teacher what their dreams are for their students. With that vision articulated, work with the teacher to create a little data assessment (or steps and checks) to get students moving toward this dream. This idea and the contrasting of big data with little data often make data more attractive to teachers. It opens them up to the possibility of exploring data inside a coaching context.

3.41: Request a Recap

If a teacher struggles with fulfilling their commitments to change, ask them to summarize what they understood from the coaching exchange. Request a verbal summary near the end of each conversation. This gives you a chance to clarify information *before* the teacher goes and practices it, and it helps them recall their action steps.

This recap also provides an opportunity to listen carefully and assess what the teacher heard. We're often surprised by the forgotten details when we request a summary. When a teacher tells you what they will do next, be prepared to add to or modify the action plan.

When we first suggest this idea to experienced coaches, they often say, "That sounds kind of patronizing, doesn't it? It doesn't sound natural." We point out that a coaching conversation isn't a casual chat between pals; it's a contrived work conversation, *a conversation with a goal*. That said, there are a couple of ways to assuage the awkwardness. First, tell the teacher up front that you'll ask them to summarize. Many times, they'll interject, "Oh, let me take notes so I remember!" which is a response we love to hear! Second, introduce the recap as something *you* need: "Just to make sure I explained everything I wanted to, will you summarize our talk?" Put the onus of weakness on you. Try this practice of requesting a summary a few times, and it'll become a common feedback step you value.

What It Looks Like in Practice

Watching a Colleague Teach

Focus Strategies:

- Observe another teacher
- Define critical thinking

Angela frequently recounts this story of a principal she worked with, who was also a strong coach. The principal observed a novice teacher teaching *Romeo and Juliet* to an honors group of students. The teacher was quite confident about their own ability to explain Shakespeare, thinking this observation provided an excellent time to impress the principal with all their knowledge. After the observation, the principal told the teacher it was commendable how much they knew about Shakespeare and that they should observe another teacher who taught the same play. The teacher was a bit surprised. The other teacher, Joey, taught the self-contained special education English class.

At first, the novice teacher thought the principal wanted them to help Joey with the content. That wasn't the case. Instead, the principal wanted the novice teacher to see an amazing teacher; the principal also planned to join the observation to pinpoint important tactics Joey used.

The principal and the novice teacher watched as Joey led students through the learning for two days. Joey asked the students to compare what was happening in the play with similar events taking place in their communities and then to analyze the characters' actions. Students read some excerpts in the Shakespearean language and some in a transliteration. The students loved the play; they dug deep into what was happening and considered the characters' maturity levels and honesty. They talked about why Shakespeare might have written a play about teenagers and what he was really saying about the community in which they lived. They argued about who was at fault for the deaths; they used text evidence to support their points. They were critical thinkers displaying a curiosity for Shakespeare. Joey's students knew hundreds of details, could explain what various Shakespearean phrases meant, and were probably quite happy that they had read the play.

This is what the novice teacher learned—that students needed to use the text to remind themselves of the details instead of memorizing all the facts, that they needed to tear apart the meaning and make connections in the text to become independent learners and develop a desire to learn more. In those two days of observing in Joey's classroom, the novice teacher reached an epiphany about the true importance of learning through critical thinking.

Fostering High-Level Thinking Every Day

 Focus Strategies:
- Define critical thinking
- Identify possibilities for integration

Keith had the honor of working with a teacher who sends students into critical thinking every day. During one set of lessons, students read two articles on a topic they were studying in science. One of the articles described a dire situation, whereas the second described a situation that might have ruined a small celebration. In both articles, a group of young people took action to help alleviate the problem. The dire situation was a drought causing a village's food supply to be limited and villagers to suffer from hunger. The other was a drought that caused a large city to impose temporary water conservation regulations, which meant a family could not fill a new pool they had constructed in anticipation of an upcoming family reunion. The lesson addressed two learning standards: *Determine two or more main ideas of a text and explain how they are supported by key details; summarize the text* and *Determine the meaning of general academic and domain-specific words and phrases in a text relevant to a grade-level topic or subject area.*

Instead of spending their time underlining the main idea once and the details twice, a practice known to kill the love of reading, students read in groups of three. Each student read silently first, and then they took turns reading a section aloud and talking with one another about what the author was saying and why the section was important. Finally, they dug down to specific sentences and words. One group looked up the word *dire* and held a rich conversation about its use and meaning. Students were seeking to answer questions such as these:

- What is the problem in both articles? What is similar and different about the ways the community addressed the issue?
- Is the problem in one story more important than the other? Why or why not?
- Which community group in the stories used a thought process most like yours? Why do you think so?
- As you reread one of the articles, consider what you would have contributed to the group in the story? What does that tell you about your critical thinking?
- Did one of the authors make you think more than the other? Why?

In discussion with the teacher, Keith learned that they often worked with their instructional coach on integrating literacy and embedding the school's focus on critical thinking.

Who Learned What?

 Focus Strategy:
- Ask simple questions

With the onset of virtual learning as a result of the COVID-19 pandemic, Angela and Keith observed several virtual classrooms with principals and coaches. After each class, the principals and coaches were excited to talk about all the great apps their teachers were using and planning to use and about how quickly the teachers had adapted to the virtual setting. At the end of the day, on several occasions, Angela and Keith asked, "Let's go back through our scripts; please tell me in each classroom who learned what?" After plowing through their lesson scripts, the leaders often looked at Angela or Keith, remarking, "I can't tell you for sure that anyone learned anything today." The conversation then moved from using the trendiest apps to what they knew about high-quality learning and how to incorporate *that* into virtual lessons.

Who Produced Thinking Independently?

 Focus Strategies:

- Focus on data
- Ask simple questions

We often demonstrate coaching conversations for coaches and principals. One day, a principal asked Keith to spend a little extra time in a 5th grade classroom. The principal observed, "We see the teacher doing some incredible things, but I think something is missing. The students' scores are not increasing as I would expect." After an observation, Keith modeled a feedback session with the teacher for the school coach and principal. The teacher used multiple engagement techniques, and, on the surface, the classroom seemed like a great place, energetic and positive. However, on further inspection, it was clear that although the teacher asked students to problem solve in groups, the teacher also gave them so much support that all the students were really doing was following a set of directions. No independent problem solving was needed in the activity.

During Keith's interaction with the teacher, they talked about the teacher's intent behind the lesson. Then they walked back through the lesson to pinpoint all the times that students *didn't* produce thinking in that lesson and then discussed how, with a few tweaks, students might demonstrate critical thinking *independent of the teacher*. The teacher fully self-reflected and planned for high-level, independent thinking from students going forward.

The Power of Academic Language

 Focus Strategy:

- Ensure teachers use academic language

The instructional leadership team initiated several goals in an alternative high school where approximately 80 percent of students had been suspended or expelled from other schools. One goal involved using academic vocabulary in conversation. Every day, the principal presented a "word of the day." Every teacher integrated the word into their daily lesson. Students were expected to use the words in writing and speaking. Every day in every class, teachers taught both domain-specific words and Tier 2 words—high-frequency, high-utility words for fluent language users (Beck et al., 2013). With Angela as their coach, the school's leadership team maintained a clear instructional focus on the use of academic language.

The schoolwide focus was highly successful. Students used conversation prompts, sentence starters, and paragraph frames to hold academic conversations and write with the domain-specific words in class. When they spoke with any adult on campus, they were to do so as though they were in a business or an academic context. For example, they learned that saying "my bad" was fine with their friends, but in class and with adults on campus, they needed to say, "I apologize" or "I made an error" instead. Angela listened one day as one student explained to the principal that they were the recipient of a scholarship to a local college. The student made it clear that they earned the scholarship because they could express themselves in their interview intelligently and articulately, thanks to the school's focus on using academic language.

Coaching from Data

 Focus Strategies:

- Focus on data
- Observe another teacher

Angela started by using these two focus strategies with a math teacher—but it didn't change a thing. The new teacher had been receiving training on the importance of student engagement. All teachers had gotten together to write the implementation goals, and they had discussed specific strategies they would try. After engaging in three coaching chats with the teacher and viewing minimal to no active student participation, Angela and the school coach observed in the teacher's class again. This time, it was clear that the teacher was no longer making any attempt to implement the strategies. Rather than trying to coach once again, they simply asked the teacher why they weren't implementing the strategies. The teacher remarked they had just "gone through the motions" to please the administrator, that it wasn't essential to have students constantly engaged in learning, and that downtime was good for students, regardless of what the coach thought. According to this teacher, student scores reflected a student's lack of motivation, not teacher issues. In the teacher's account, the coach heard an internal bias that "these students" needed less formality in their teacher.

The school coach and Angela explained that the student engagement goals weren't based on opinion. They reviewed the research the teacher had read previously and arranged for the teacher to observe a social studies teacher with them. The teacher reluctantly but willingly agreed. The social studies teacher proved to be a student engagement superstar and taught many of the same students the math teacher did. In the social studies classroom, the math teacher saw many of those students behaving like scholars, attending to their studies, and discussing their learning.

Afterward, the teacher admitted that the students were showing more attention to their learning in the social studies class than in the math class. Nonetheless, the teacher made it clear that what the social studies teacher did was not "their kind of teaching." The teacher made some effort to change but left at the end of the year to teach elsewhere. Sometimes, successful coaching helps a teacher see that they're simply not in the right place.

Coaches, Consider This...

- Jot down the content area or academic instructional practice that is most challenging for you to coach.
- How might you strengthen your knowledge in the area you listed?
- What can you do to stay abreast of the latest content knowledge in the area that you coach?

4

Coaching Social-Emotional Instruction

We begin our discussion of coaching social-emotional instruction with the topic of classroom management. In our experience, this is the second most frequently coached topic of all. The primary objectives in this area are instructing students to be productive members of the learning community and developing their emotions appropriately in the classroom. Hattie (2012) made it evident that highly productive teachers are highly skilled at identifying instructional strategies, including affective skills. Using powerful explanatory tactics, providing explicit feedback, and arranging climates conducive to learning are crucial components of building positive social-emotional outcomes with students.

The powerful emotional reactions of both students and teachers often complicate the coaching of classroom management. Kim and colleagues (2019) identified emotional calmness as a trait of effective teachers. Accordingly, this chapter offers coaches suggestions for helping the teacher and the student find and maintain calm in classrooms. Both Costa and colleagues (2016) and Kim note that dynamic teachers seek excellence in their practice—and that applies to social-emotional as well as to academic learning.

If the teacher you coach struggles with building relationships with students or with any other component of classroom management, cruise through the strategies in this chapter for what might work best with the teacher's personality or the class's characteristics.

Researcher	Effective Teacher Traits or Dispositions Related to Social-Emotional Instruction
Costa et al. (2016)	• Skillfulness: desires to be professionally explicit, elegant, precise • Interdependence: values relationships with others, desires community and reciprocity
Hattie (2012)	• Creates an optimal classroom climate for learning • Monitors learning and provides feedback • Believes all students can reach the success criteria • Influences a wide range of student outcomes not solely limited to test scores
Kim et al. (2019)	• Conscientiousness: ambitious, highly responsible, organized • Emotional stability: maintains high levels of calm and tolerance of stress

Strategies

4.1: Start Small

Sometimes teachers are overwhelmed when it comes to building and repairing relationships with students. Suggest that the teacher start by learning their students' names or tweaking one common redirection. Target relationship building with one or two students at a time (see the next strategy for some ideas). Begin with a couple approaches, and build on those tiny successes. Typically, after starting slowly and narrowly, the teacher will be able to implement subsequent work more rapidly.

4.2: Build Relationships with Students

Provide the teacher with relatively easy strategies for building relationships with students. Here are some examples:

- Share personal anecdotes directly related to the teaching topic.
- Tell students how you struggled or worked on learning the content at hand; this might sound like, "Here's how I struggled to find success when I learned _____," *not* "I'm still not good at _____."
- Use "*I* messages" when communicating with students (Gordon & Burch, 2003). For example, "You say you feel _____. I felt similarly when _____. I found that, over time, I _____."
- Admit—and celebrate—your mistakes. The teacher could remark, "Yesterday, I was very unhappy with you all when we were lining up for the assembly. This happened because I thought I had explained the routine too many times and lost my patience. I am sorry for that. I'm going to work on telling you when I'm upset more appropriately in the future. Let's do our chant for learning from mistakes. On three, 'Mistakes help us learn!'" Coach the teacher to make up their own mantra that fits their content and age group (Dweck, 2016).
- Share something new you're working on learning.
- Share a personal goal. For example, "I'm working on returning your graded essays within a week" or "I'm working on transitioning us to recess more quickly, so we get all our time on the playground."
- Conduct class meetings or community builders, and make sure you participate in the activities along with the students.

- Observe details about the students as learners. For example, how do they approach problems, practice skills, articulate thinking, or relate concepts? For more details about this tactic, see the strategy *consider all aspects of students as learners* in Chapter 6, as well as the implementation story "Spreading Praise" at the end of this chapter.
- Share your interests with students, especially when they relate to the day's learning.
- Try to find moments to laugh with students.

4.3: Repair Student Relationships

Brainstorm methods for repairing relationships. If the teacher needs to mend a relationship, perhaps after a challenging incident with a student, ask them to consider trying one of the following.

- Deliver a clear apology to the student. Tell the student what you did wrong and what you'll do in the future to correct it.
- Admit errors in teaching, as in "You know what, I was wrong when I said _____."
- Restart with a clean slate. This move involves no direct verbal interaction with the student; it's a mental and an emotional perspective on the teacher's part. In other words, once the teacher resolves a negative incident with a student, the next day start fresh. Try to hold positive expectations for the student without dwelling on past errors. It takes practice to get into this mindset consistently, but it's doable.
- After a challenging encounter, work to separate the person from the behavior. Say, "You know, I like you. I'm glad you're my student. I'm just not OK with that behavior" or "You're much more than that outburst that happened yesterday." (This interaction is similar to recommendations in Jim Fay's *Creating a Love and Logic School Culture* [2011].)

- Once emotions are calmer, revisit the issue, starting a conversation with one of the following:
    - » "I want to talk about what happened this morning. Here's what I wanted to mention but didn't."
    - » "Let's talk about the disagreement we had yesterday."
    - » "I want to make sure you know our relationship is OK."
- Work on amends. After the incident, when everyone involved is less emotional, explain the following to the student: "What happened yesterday hurt me (or another person or some property). One way to deal with that is to make a sincere apology or repair or replace damaged property. What can you do today to fix what happened? Do you want ideas?" Many teachers report that this tactic is more potent than forcing students to apologize when they're still upset right after a difficult situation.

4.4: Eliminate Sarcasm

Sarcasm kills relationships (Saphier et al., 2018). After a couple decades of advising principals and coaches on how best to coach around sarcasm, we compiled a list of our best tips and turned them into five steps:

1. **Gather data from the classroom**—that is, direct teacher quotes that reveal sarcasm. Then prepare for a one-on-one conversation with the teacher. Be explicit and use direct quotes; don't infer with remarks like "It feels sarcastic sometimes when you respond" or "The tone in your corrections needs to be warmer." If you need help with this step, get a colleague to go with you to observe and collect data. Compare notes with each other to make sure you understand what you are and are not coding as sarcasm.

2. **Point out the evidence of sarcasm** from the collected data. Share *precisely* what the teacher stated. Contrast that with what the teacher was intending or trying to communicate. The more examples you have, the better. For example, a student asks what page they should be working on when the teacher has already stated the page number four times. The teacher responds, "If you brought your brain to school today, you'd know what page we're on." In reality, the teacher was irritated because the student didn't listen, and maybe this was the 18th time the student did this in the past three days.

3. **Define** *sarcasm.* Explain that it's student correction with scorn; it's veiled teacher anger. The word's ill intent emanates from the Greek root, which means "to tear away flesh with the teeth."

4. **Discuss the problematic effects of sarcasm.** At least three issues merit consideration:

   - It's far preferable to use direct, explicit language with students, as opposed to indirect communication (Hattie & Clarke, 2019; Stone & Heen, 2014).
   - Students need to hear and see models of acceptable ways of communicating anger in the classroom. Offer strategies for how students and the teacher may express anger in class. Use other prosocial skills instruction, such as ignoring, counting to 10, using an "*I* message," and so on.
   - Explain the effect of sarcasm on bystanders and its hidden damage to relationships with shy or powerless students. Other students are listening even when they're not the intended target. Remind the teacher that dual-language learners may be translating everything the teacher says literally. Have them imagine how something sarcastic they say might feel—if it were directed to them.

5. **Work with the teacher on a communication plan** to practice alternatives to sarcasm.

Be ready for pushback if there's disagreement from the teacher. For example, the teacher might tell you that this is a method of building relationships and that the student understands their humor. Some teachers may disagree that sarcasm is veiled anger. Regardless of the definition of the word, some adults don't view the issue as problematic. Others view sarcasm as central to their identity and cannot imagine functioning in their role as teachers differently.

Stand your ground. We're continually amazed to hear educators describe sarcasm as an appropriate practice. Although it's predominantly an issue with teachers in the upper grades, we've heard teachers use sarcasm with students as young as 4 years old. Some of the earliest research on sarcasm and its adverse effects on students dates back almost a century to the 1920s (Briggs, 1928; Laird, 1923). Label sarcasm as an ineffective, needless communication strategy for building relationships with students, provide a myriad of other communication tactics more appropriate to use, and ask for the sarcasm to stop. People often make a change after thinking about something for a long time. Although you may not always get immediate results, you will at least generate teacher speculation on the topic.

4.5: Coach Care

Teach the concept of caring as a teacher's ethical or professional responsibility, as described by Nel Noddings (2013) in *Caring*. Ethical care is similar to what a nurse or social worker demonstrates as part of their job. Brainstorm opportunities for establishing care, such as greeting students, showing personal interest, using a student's preferred name, giving a personal descriptive note of appreciation, planning targeted conversations, scheduling targeted academic feedback, and so on. Draft a plan to include caring acts into weekly teacher interactions with students. Ask the teacher to write down what they'll do when and with which student.

4.6: Show That Care Affects Academics

Share research on the power of building relationships with students and the effect of that effort on academic achievement. Locate research indicating that powerful learning revolves around developmentally supportive relationships (Darling-Hammond et al., 2020; Saphier et al., 2018). Saphier devotes an entire chapter in his book—Chapter 15—to that topic.

4.7: Conduct a 30-Day Experiment

Encourage the teacher to experiment for 30 days with a specific caring strategy. This might include teaching the student various social-emotional skills, role-playing, noticing positive attributes, learning something new about the student each day, or conducting one-on-one check-ins. Have them target a midrange student—one with whom they struggle to relate but who doesn't present significant behavioral issues. Not starting with the most challenging student proves pivotal with this strategy. Often, the teacher builds up a great deal of ill will toward their challenging student; there's so much negative momentum flowing around the relationship that it's hard to buck the teacher's negative train of thought. Starting with a less challenging student offers a little more room for success with this approach.

After experimenting with the first student and gaining a little success and confidence in the strategy, ask the teacher to target a more challenging student—a student they don't care for and with whom they're encountering significant issues. Teachers are frequently shocked when this strategy proves to be the only intervention they needed with the student.

4.8: Use Guided Imagery

Have the teacher visualize a student who is challenging for them. Then ask them to imagine the student next year, a few years from now, or several years from now at a milestone in their life—receiving an award, entering high school, graduating college, getting a promotion, or getting married. That now-former student is thanking this teacher with a note, an editorial, or a public speech. Ask the teacher, "What do you hope this student says you did for them?" Push them to explain and be specific about the student's remarks.

Afterward, ask them to debrief how that *felt*. Then make a plan. What actions can the teacher take tomorrow to make those future words come true? For more details about this maneuver, check out *mental imagery* in *The Skillful Teacher* (Saphier et al., 2018). If you're anxious about trying this method, practice first with other coaches or a friendly critic.

You can also have the teacher respond to your verbal or written prompts in writing. Then they can discuss the effect this had on them with you or with a small group of teachers. We've found activities like this one work well when the teacher is frustrated with a student or needs to get in touch with the softer, more heartfelt side of teaching.

4.9: Simply Say It

If you've inferred a direction, offered suggestions, provided related readings, or tried reflective coaching to no avail, just tell the teacher what needs to happen. Sometimes the shortest route is the best one. Be warm-hearted, be humble, and just say it: "You need to lower your voice; you're yelling at students." "You cannot physically manage a student." "I don't get your classroom directions about cooperative group expectations." "Students *can* produce this behavior in your classroom." Think of it as a gift you give; you may be the first person to be this explicit with the teacher. Try other approaches first and don't overrely on this method, but use it when needed. To see this strategy in action, read the implementation story "Getting Off the Rolling Chair" at the end of this chapter.

4.10: Forecast Care

Intentionally use the words *care, love,* or *appreciation* in conversations with the teacher. "I know you care about this student. You demonstrated your care for your students with that well-crafted lesson." Some teachers never heard themselves described as caring or appreciative as educators. Even consider praising the *approximation* of such dispositions, such as "I noticed you keep a tidy room; that's a very caring act you show for your students." "You took a great deal of pride in selecting suitable reading materials for that unit; you care a great deal about your teaching and, by extension, your students." "I notice you didn't reprimand the student for not having a pen; you simply picked up an extra one from your desk and handed it to them. That was very generous of you." Find something that comes close to aspects of care, label it as such, and praise it. With forecasting, you're laying out the possibility that care, nurture, or love exists inside the teacher, even when you don't see much of it. Over time, more evidence of this disposition may arise; if so, label it. In the interim, just start by implying it, no matter how minimal the evidence is.

4.11: Rekindle Professional Motivation

See if you can unearth the teacher's motivation, and link that intention to students' social or emotional needs. Ask, "If money were not an issue, would you still be doing this work?" Depending on the response, ask the teacher how they might get their passion back into the classroom or with students ... or ask why they first got into teaching. If you see that the teacher is passionate about the topic but not about *teaching* the topic, ask them to brainstorm ways to get the students to be as passionate about the subject as they are. Say, "Obviously, you have a great passion for music (or their subject); how can we get some of that love for music to the students?" or "What got you excited about this topic the first time you encountered it? Let's use that with your students." Sometimes this technique connects the teacher to students' social and emotional needs around content.

4.12: Use Student Heart

Engage the teacher's students in a caring activity, such as writing thank-you letters to the teacher, producing artwork describing what they like about the teacher, creating a teacher gratitude video, or listing their favorite things about their teacher—anything that touches the teacher on a personal level. Do it in secret for maximum effect, and present it formally to the teacher in front of students. As a coach, ensure all the content is positive and encouraging for the teacher. Teachers are often surprised to find out how much, how well, and with how much precision students think about them.

4.13: Use Student Disclosure

Help the teacher gain empathy and make personal connections with the students. Engage the teacher's students in responding in writing to the following prompt: "One thing I wish my teacher knew about me is _____." Present the vignettes as a book to the teacher. Teachers struggling with social and emotional instruction are often quite surprised to discover personal, significant facts about their students with this activity.

4.14: Shadow a Student

Have the teacher shadow a challenging student for a day and document how much care, love, appreciation, and personal interest staff and students offer the youngster. The point is to build empathy for what the student encounters over the course of a school day. Afterward, ask them what they learned from the experience. This practice works well for academic prowess as well.

4.15: Ask Reflective Questions

For work on social and emotional instruction, consider asking teachers these questions:

- "You mentioned the student was defiant; what are your feelings around that?" Probing the teacher's emotions may help clarify their assumptions or definitions around an issue. Perhaps the teacher views a student's developmental defiance as a moral flaw, as personally disrespectful, as manipulative, or as abnormal. Getting at the teacher's understanding of the root cause of a behavior may help you move the teacher to more developmentally appropriate interventions.

- "How might you appropriately demonstrate care, concern, or appreciation for students in your course or class?"

- "How comfortable are you talking to this student about racism, sexism, homophobia, or other biases? How can you talk about that student's diagnosed disabilities in a way that is empowering for them?"

- "You've clearly stated the student's misbehavior. In what context would that same behavior be a positive attribute? Can you use that awareness in your classroom to help redirect the student?"

- "How could you word this differently to communicate to the student what you truly intended?"

- "Picture yourself as the student at that moment. What is going through your mind? What are you feeling?"

- "Speaking of this student, what do we know, in general, about the effect of racial, sexual, or ethnic identity development on them at this age? Is that relevant to this situation?"

4.16: Use Teacher Role-Play

Have the teacher role-play caring, as opposed to uncaring, teacher words and actions. First, ask the teacher to repeat statements, directions, corrections, or feedback you heard them provide in the classroom. Next, give a brief context; for example, a student slumps in their chair, scrolls on their phone, and completes no writing 10 minutes into the task. Then have the teacher role-play how they would redirect the student. Conduct a few rounds; before each round, add a bit of detail to change the context. Use prompts similar to these:

- "Speak as you would to your most annoying student."
- "Speak as though you're talking to a student you enjoy seeing but who is just having an off day."
- "Now act as though you were talking to a colleague you know is struggling with many personal issues."
- "Pretend this student is visiting today and that you know little or nothing about them."
- "Give this feedback as though you knew this student was worried about their mother's illness."

Debrief the feelings surrounding each comment. Then develop a plan to help the teacher check their intention and make their redirects more caring, or at least more neutral, before they deliver them live in the classroom.

4.17: Use Coach Role-Play

Instead of the teacher leading the role-play, the coach leads a scenario in which they move from uncaring to caring teacher words and actions. First, use statements, directions, corrections, or feedback you heard the teacher provide in the classroom; for example, model the verbal redirect delivered with a cold or an angry tone. Pretend to be the teacher, with the teacher pretending to be the student.

Then model the same verbal exchange with a warm tone and positive intent. Next, ask the teacher which delivery felt better and why. Finally, ask them to practice a few rounds of doing the same thing you just modeled. In Monterey County, California, learning director and preschool coach Laura Xochitl Valdez Chavez demonstrates this in teacher feedback sessions. Laura first learned the tactic from teaching parenting classes, then found it worked well with coaching teachers.

4.18: Track Names

While observing in-person or virtual teaching, keep a running log of which students' names are used and how; review the list with the teacher and ask for their reaction. They're often surprised to discover who was left out. Help the teacher think about what the patterns might tell them. Explain the importance of using names and of students hearing their names attached to essential learning. Print a student roster, put it in a sheet protector, and use a whiteboard marker to indicate every time the teacher uses a student's name positively and attaches it to meaningful learning. For example, "Claire, I can see you're writing complete sentences!" "Absolom, could you remind the class about how to use the Pythagorean Theorem?"

4.19: Optimize Physical Space

Show the teacher how to use physical proximity to move closer to students for relationship purposes. Tell the primary teacher to sit down on the floor with students in centers. Ask the teacher in upper grades not to place the most challenging student farthest from them. In a room full of desks, physically show the teacher where the best vantage points are for standing in the room to quickly scan the students. Have the teacher use more, not less, proximity for challenging students and for students who are not immediately likable.

4.20: Signal Positive Student Behaviors

Suppose the teacher sees no positive behaviors from a student. Offer to observe the student; whenever you see them correctly following the routine or rules, signal the teacher. The teacher's job is then to describe the action or praise the student. This highlighting helps them see the potentially missed moments when the student engages appropriately. It's easy for us to generalize challenging student behavior—just see that negative aspect of them—and fail to see their efforts at cooperation. "The Coach's Arm (Nearly) Falls Off," an implementation story in Chapter 2, addresses this strategy.

4.21: Identify Triggers

Ask the teacher what student behaviors push their buttons—ones that truly and personally offend or trigger them. For example, some teachers find threats offensive, and others hate foul language; teachers vary in their reactions to student behavior they consider out of bounds. Then empower the teacher to manage dealing with that particular behavior. Tell them to plan for that inevitable occurrence. Explore five or six strategies for responding to the behavior; many are included in this book. Practice reacting to the behavior until the teacher finds a neutral, or possibly warm, disposition when responding to the issue. This way, they're prepared, not caught off guard, when the behavior arises.

4.22: Rework Reprimands

Take a few common corrections the teacher delivered, and generate ideas for turning those corrections into "Feel, Felt, Found" messages, a tactic from *Teacher Effectiveness Training* (Gordon & Burch, 2003). For example, "You say you feel _____. I felt similarly when _____. I found that over time, I _____." There is no shortage of ideas for gaining and maintaining student concentration (e.g., McCarney & Wunderlich, 2014; Saphier et al., 2018), but one way to rework reprimands includes having students restate the correct rule or routine for their current misbehavior. Another approach separates the child from behavior or depersonalizes the reprimand and engages student reflection. For example, rather than say "DeMarco! Give that back!" a preschool teacher might instead ask, "DeMarco, how do you think that makes Shelby feel when you take that away from her?"

4.23: Focus on What You Want

Help the teacher rehearse or write out how to focus on student behaviors they *want* to see (Bailey, 2015). Many teachers quickly focus on what they *don't* want to see, with comments such as "Stop running," "Stop talking," and "You can't use that word"; they neglect to see the potential of focusing on the desired behavior. This subtle yet powerful move reframes comments to focus on what action is needed in the moment. For example, "It's time for you to use your words," "You need to apologize," "Open your book," "Start writing," "Walk!" "Eyes forward, Marcio." This approach may require you to do guided practice with the teacher, writing out sample redirections.

When you first ask teachers what they want to see in a student, they may not be able to articulate it. It may take a few attempts, and you may need to help them voice their desired outcome, but stay focused and help the teacher cross this bridge. Getting them to verbalize what they need to see helps them with two issues: (1) directions in the classroom, and (2) the next strategy, *teach prosocial skills*.

4.24: Teach Prosocial Skills

If the teacher relies solely on rewards, punishments, or token societies (a whole-class process where the teacher provides points or prizes for desired behaviors) for classroom management, introduce them to strategies for teaching the social skills they want to see from the students. Many authors provide a wide range of such practices instead of simply expecting students to know beforehand the social norms of the class (e.g., Bailey, 2011, 2015; Bilmes, 2012; Curwin et al., 2008; Divinyi, 2010; Dweck, 2016; Fay, 2011; Gordon & Burch, 2003; Lemov, 2021; McCarney & Wunderlich, 2014; Saphier et al., 2018; Smith, 2004; Sprick, 2012; Wadhwa, 2016; Wilson, 2012). A few common approaches to social-emotional instruction include these:

- During class meetings or one-on-one sessions, have students role-play challenging situations. For example, students take turns playing the victim, bully, bystander, rule breaker, and so on. Role-play is a dynamic and straightforward way for students to practice dealing with strong emotions in a non-threatening setting. You might practice both examples and nonexamples.

- Produce, post, and practice examples of targeted social skills with T-charts or anchor charts. Figure 4.1 shows a social and work skills chart from an upper school math teacher at Frankfurt International School in Germany. Students use this during group or cooperative learning activities. All students take specific jobs and complete specific tasks. Each team provides evidence that team members helped one another as well.

- During a class meeting or other social instruction time, conduct a teacher think-aloud, with the teacher taking an angry student's point of view. For example, "I'm thinking about what happens if I hit that student. I know I'll probably get in trouble. What else could I do? I could rip up that mean note they sent me, but that would probably get me in trouble instead of them. I think I could tell them in a strong voice to *stop*. Or, if I think they're going to start an argument, I could ask an adult for help. I think I'll take a deep breath and then decide."

- Post photographs of common expectations, such as lining up or transitioning between centers or stations. Verbally highlight or simply point to the visual expectation. The visuals become silent teachers in the classroom. We often see this idea in elementary schools. Nevertheless, one high school chemistry teacher, exasperated from reminding students of appropriate labwear, took a photo of a student fully suited up, posted it at each lab, and simply pointed to the image to remind students to put their goggles or lab coat on.

- Describe what you *want* to see with comments such as these: "I know you're open to criticism." "You're a caring friend." "I'm sure you like to learn new ideas." "This part you'll love." "You'll hear this easily." "You're flexible, I can tell." "You're a problem solver." "You have a kind heart."

- Conduct explicit instruction on the desired behavior, an "I do, we do, you do" lesson in which you start by modeling instruction on a given topic, students practice the skill or concept with the teacher, and students finish by completing that learning independently. For example, with secondary students, provide models of appropriate emails to the teacher or practice together how to move safely among labs or centers in order to be more explicit with prosocial skills.

- Plan kindness rituals. For elementary students, you might have a box into which students put kind notes describing nice things they witnessed other students doing; the teacher might draw a few from the box to read to the class daily (Bailey, 2015). At the secondary level, the teacher might hold quick rounds of verbal appreciation as students wrap up and prepare for the bell at the end of the period.

Figure 4.1   Social and Work Skills Anchor Chart

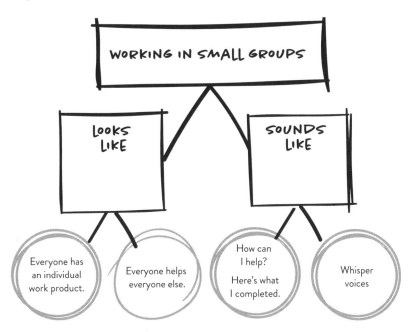

4.25: Multiply the Management Bag of Tricks

If the teacher relies on a single, ineffective practice for classroom management—such as yelling, threatening, and so on—introduce them to various approaches, but only two or three at a time. For example, show them how to offer choices, set goals, or set up a one-person workstation. Then practice the strategies with the teacher. Watch them display the practice live with students, and provide feedback out of earshot. Introduce two or three more techniques the following week. Find numerous classroom management strategies in *The Skillful Teacher* (Saphier et al., 2018), *Creating a Love and Logic School Culture* (Fay, 2011), *Teacher's Encyclopedia of Behavior Management* (Sprick, 2012), or books specific to elementary teachers from Becky Bailey (2011, 2015). Start to collect short lists of productive strategies for the age group at your site. Parse out ideas in small doses, practice them with the teacher, and focus on the teacher's prompt enactment.

4.26: Suggest Calming Strategies for Teachers

If the teacher struggles to stay calm when dealing with a challenging student or situation, discuss procedures for calming themselves *before* they deliver a consequence or response. In training, we surveyed educators about how they compose themselves before managing students, and here are a few of their recommendations:

- Count to 10 silently.
- Say, "I'm not responding to that right now. I'm too angry. I'll deal with that later."
- Look up and tell yourself, "The ceiling is white." Then look down and think, "The floor is beige." Then speak out loud.
- Press or rub your feet on the floor.
- Mentally repeat a calming mantra before speaking. These are some of our favorites:
  - » Patience, patience, plus humor
  - » Always begin from caring.
  - » I'm a good teacher; what can I teach in this situation?
  - » I can meet this student's needs.
  - » Smile, breathe, love, make change.
- Look around the room and silently count five objects. Physically touch three things. Take two breaths. Then speak.
- Take several deep breaths.
- Mentally appeal to the universe, God, or a higher power before speaking.
- As you walk toward the student, repeatedly say to yourself, "I don't know what I'll say. I know I'll be calm; I know I'll be calm."

- Keep a personal amulet—a small figurine, piece of jewelry, or tiny photograph of your child—around your neck or on your desk to help anchor you. Touch it before you speak.

4.27: Reflect on Personal Experiences

Have the teacher reflect in writing about their own emotional encounters with their teachers—their best and worst experiences. Then ask them how, with their current students, they can embody the best and avoid the worst of what they encountered. For example, "How did a previous teacher of yours communicate care to you or other classmates? How can you make that happen with your students?" or "In what ways did a previous teacher communicate low expectations to you about your behavior? How did that make you feel? What steps can you take to make sure this doesn't happen for your students?"

4.28: Engage in Out-of-Sight Thoughts

Suggest the teacher maintain positive or productive thoughts about the challenging student *when the student is not in front of them*. For example, they might imagine powerful interactions with the student while preparing for work, during their daily commute, or as they mark up the student's writing. Also, disengage from negative discussions about the student with other staff members. If other adults verbally disparage the student, pivot the conversation to focus on the student's attributes, or find a way to politely leave the conversation. Some people claim that complaining to others about a student provides valuable venting, but the research reveals that too much time airing complaints can potentially lead to depression (Yoon et al., 2017).

One teacher reported a successful tactic for decreasing negative talk about students. When someone begins to complain about one of their students, they ask, "What strategies did you use to help the student with _____ (whatever the adult is complaining about)?" They often need to repeat the question a couple of times before the person finally stops the conversation because they have no constructive ideas to offer. Sometimes the questioning teacher persists, saying, "Really, I'm curious to know what you tried because I want to see if *I* need to use that strategy with the same student." Successful or not, they're pushing the focus of the conversation to solutions instead of just regurgitating the problem.

4.29: Teach Student Self-Regulation

If the teacher struggles to manage a student's emotional outbursts, have them study how to teach self-regulation. Bailey's (2011) book, *Managing Emotional Mayhem,* provides a solid starting place. If the student cannot manage their emotions, and the teacher and student are safe, suggest the teacher try one or a combination of the following calming strategies:

- Physically describe to the student what you see them doing: "You're looking down. Tears are on your cheeks. Your arms are crossed. Your breathing is short and fast." You can even demonstrate this at the same time. Often, the student physically relaxes. Then you can suggest they might be upset or angry or possibly ready to talk about what happened. We learned this skill from Becky Bailey (2011, 2015).
- Notice something peculiar and objective about the student's appearance: "Did you see that your left shoelace is untied?" "Is that purple magic marker on your arm, or is it a freckle?" "Your bow is about to fall out of your hair," and so on. Sometimes, the student's focus shifts. At that point, you might be able to talk about the topic that upset them.

- Ask the student to take deep breaths, stretch, or take a brisk walk with you, which engages large muscles or deep breathing. The breathing and stretching tactics work well, especially if the teacher has included these practices throughout the school day.

- With older students, ask the student to self-assess their problem (Santos, 2017). Is this a major, medium, or small problem? Mental self-assessment may cause emotional relaxation.

- Request a tiny movement. Say, "Stand up." "Walk with me to the door." "Pick up your sweater." "Take my hand." "Help me _____." This may get the student into the flow of moving with you and mentally agreeing with you; you may then be able to shift to problem solving the issue they're upset about. Once, kneeling to help an 8-year-old calm down from an episode of screaming, Keith pleaded, "Oh, lord! You have to help this old man get up. My knees hurt." In a jiffy, the student settled down and began pulling Keith up off the floor. Then, with their hands firmly clasped because the student was dragging Keith forward, the two walked into the hallway to discuss what had happened to upset the student.

Remind the teacher to focus on one issue at a time. For example, if the student hits another student, then throws materials when you reprimand them, focus on the hitting. Later, well after the incident and once they are calm, follow up on how they handled the materials.

4.30: Structure Classroom Transitions

Be aware that most management issues occur during class transitions—at the beginning of class, at the end of class, or moving from one activity to another. Help the teacher produce tightly structured procedures for these times. The teacher might craft a script for what they will do and say during these times; have them practice transitions with students, encourage the use of a timer, and set goals for shorter and more precise movement in transitions. Model a tightly structured transition for the teacher, such as students smoothly moving from independent work to cooperative groups within 90 seconds. Observe and provide feedback to the teacher *only on transitions.* If possible, give them feedback live as they practice in the classroom through a signal, whisper, text, or sign. Suggest the teacher use color or directional signs to help them remember the expectations; in preschool, this might look like a blue tape line that leads students to the classroom bathroom or the sink.

4.31: Pump Joy into the Room

Work with the teacher to insert moments of fun, joy, or levity into the learning environment (Lemov, 2021; Saphier et al., 2018). Walk the teacher through how to use appropriate humor, ways to insert cheers or chants, when to take tiny academic breaks, and how to deploy brief community builders that fit their students, content, and teaching style.

4.32: Clarify Directions

Some teachers set up their own management problems with inexplicit classroom directions. Script or record several examples of the teacher's directions, and review them using the following list. Lemov (2021) provides reliable information on the attributes of explicit directions. Clear, brisk, positive, precise directions cure many ills in the weakly managed classroom. We use several of Lemov's ideas, as well as our own tips, to suggest the following criteria for clear classroom directions:

- Have a consistent signal (such as a chime or noisemaker) and spot in the classroom (beside the document camera or to the left of the front of the class) for delivering directions.

- Be explicit. Instead of remarking, "Listen up," try, "Your eyes are on me." Avoid vague phrases such as, "Pay attention," "Focus," "Get it together," and so on.

- Give no more than three or four steps (Cowan, 2000). If you need more steps, complete the first few steps, check that everyone finished, and then provide another set of three or four steps. We've found this works with everyone, from preschoolers to high schoolers.

- Instead of describing behavior you don't want to see—such as, *"Don't* look at your neighbor" or *"Stop playing* with your pencil"—say, "Eyes on me; pencils on your desk; smiles on your faces."

- Give the steps in sequential order. Say, "Open your novel, use a pen to complete the handout questions, and put the completed work in the bin. Go." Don't ramble like this: "Open your novel. Oh, before I forget, hand me your permission slips. Put the slips in the bin with your completed handouts. Finish your handouts using the novel. Remember to use a pen." Pay attention to this detail of sequencing in coaching. If needed, script what you hear the teacher do. Then work on small sets of written steps in coaching sessions to help the teacher establish a habit of sequential directions.

- Check direction steps during the delivery of the steps. For example, you might say the following: "Hold up the pen." "Point to your neighbor's page number 27; that's the page you need to open." "Point to the fire extinguisher next to your lab, everyone."

If needed, have teachers script a few sets of directions and practice them with you.

4.33: Group Coach for Social-Emotional Skills

Bring a team together to talk about a common social-emotional issue—for example, disrespectful treatment of other students at recess. Have the teachers discuss it as clinically as possible. How often does it occur? When and where is disrespect most prominent? What are the disrespectful students attempting to gain? Are they successful? How might those students meet their needs *without* being rude? Let the teachers role-play a typical situation and discuss their own emotions. Assuming students may experience similar sentiments, how might these feelings affect learning? Have the teachers determine creative solutions to the problem. Offering a long, analytical process similar to this helps teachers relax around the issue they're facing so they might better problem solve the situation.

4.34: Use Social Data (Stories)

Collect examples of how teacher care translates to students, and use them one-on-one, in small teams, and in large-group training. Pull together stories of how teacher care improved a student's academic success or social and emotional well-being. Often, teachers take actions of care and love that they never even realize had an effect. In the following example, a secondary student writes in an online forum about the effect their band teacher had on them in online learning during the recent pandemic:

> Every day, my band teacher would ask us all to put in the Zoom chat how we were feeling from 1 to 5: 1 is not great, and 5 is amazing! I've been putting 1s and 2s because I've been feeling sad and lonely lately. Because it's band, I just assumed he probably didn't read any of those because the class has 80 students. However, today when he put us into breakout rooms, he told me that he noticed that I haven't been feeling my A-game lately and that if I ever needed to talk, I could always stay after class or have a meeting with him. I laughed it off because I didn't want to be a burden on him. Anyway,

just that small interaction of him noticing, even though we're in a huge class, just made me feel like there's always someone out there. My parents always laugh whenever I talk about my feelings, and having my teacher saying that they're here for me brightened my day so much. I'm just so grateful for all the teachers out there who care for their students. It's difficult online, and I thank you for doing your best to connect with your students. Now I feel like I'm at a solid 3 or 4. (saddestmonkey, 2020)

Collect personal accounts like this to remind teachers of their potential power to promote social-emotional health among the students under their care.

4.35: Introduce the 2×10 Strategy

This strategy involves having the teacher talk to a target student for at least two minutes each day for 10 days in a row (Honsinger & Brown, 2019; Wlodkowski, 1983). The conversation is brief, the teacher solicits the student's voice, and the topic is positive; try not to focus on negative issues the student may be displaying. Let the teacher know that in the beginning, the student may be reluctant to speak up. Encourage the teacher to persevere through this phase; they should see student engagement within a few days. Debrief with the teacher the nature of the student relationship after one or two rounds of 2×10; remember, a round is 10 whole school days.

4.36: Express the Nobility of Education

Add words and phrases to your coaching language that communicate the nobility and privilege of being an educator: "It's a privilege to work with these students." "This work is very challenging, but at the same time, it's an honor to know we're entrusted with the care and education of these young people." "I know it may not feel like it right now, but you've entered a noble profession. I believe in time you'll see that's true." Adopting this kind of language in the coaching environment lends significance and professionalism to education and potentially fosters more respect for students.

4.37: Use Data from Others

Conduct a 360-degree review of the teacher you're coaching with feedback from multiple sources. Help the teacher understand how the school or team interprets that teacher's effect by soliciting input from colleagues, parents, students, and other staff. The coach can construct a simple survey, completed anonymously, about strengths and weaknesses of communication or affective skills to review with the teacher. For ideas on how to mitigate a teacher's emotional response to the feedback, consider the following: engage the teacher in setting up the process, be clear about who maintains access to the data, review the data in person with the teacher, and consider other approaches (such as those covered in Chapter 5).

4.38: Do This Every Day, All the Time

Request that the teacher make the necessary change *at the next available opportunity* or at *every available opportunity*. In particular, teachers need to perform strategies multiple times, perhaps 7–10 times, before they see a change in students or before switching to another approach with social and emotional work.

What It Looks Like in Practice

Spreading Praise

Focus Strategies:
- Repair student relationships
- Multiply the management bag of tricks

- Group coach for social-emotional skills
- Reflect on personal experiences
- Eliminate sarcasm
- Use teacher role-play
- Ask reflective questions
- Teach prosocial skills

In a small New Mexico school district, Angela had the opportunity to observe in K–12 classrooms and coach the leaders with *repair student relationships, multiply the management bag of tricks,* and *group coach for social-emotional skills.* Angela and the school coaches observed together and were struck by the enormous differences in the positive talk as they moved through the grades. In kindergarten, praise was effusive. It was exhausting just keeping up with how many times the teacher dispensed targeted feedback and praise: "Wow, look at Jolie, Trevor, Sunshine, Neveah, and Burt. They're all sitting and keeping their bodies to themselves in the circle!" "I heard Polly tell her partner that we were reading about great herons because they're an essential part of our ecosystem. Way to use our vocabulary!" The positive appreciation went on and on. It followed similarly in 1st and 2nd grade, with teachers referring to students as "The Littles." But something changed in 3rd grade. For teachers to congratulate them, students had to go a bit beyond the expected. Reminders began to replace the positives: "So, Miguel, what's our classroom expectation? Yes, you *know* you have to sit up when you're listening."

Then, in 4th and 5th grade, it was as though the student began to disappear; the learning content now took center stage. We heard an occasional "Lei, thank you for turning around" or "Jeremiah, that was a good question," but the detailed upbeat narration had dissolved. The appreciative comments continued to wane in 6th grade; by 7th and 8th grade, neither teachers nor students seemed to realize the importance of positive feedback. When the comments occurred (rarely), they were almost embarrassing. By high school, teachers had replaced praise with sarcastic humor: "Wow, you turned this in on time! Are you feeling OK?" and "Let me mark this down; Pete asked a question *on the topic!*"

Angela and coaches from all grade levels began by analyzing the data, which included direct quotes from teachers at each grade level. The brainstorming followed this two-step format:

1. **Is this a problem?** Coaches spent time researching the effects of positive feedback and interactions. Their decision was a resounding "Yes, this is a problem for our students!"

2. **What misconceptions do teachers have about older students and positive interactions?** Using the strategy *reflect on personal experiences*, the coaches realized that adult embarrassment about being singled out for positive feedback often stemmed from their high school years, where positive feedback was a rare occurrence. Focusing on the strategy *eliminate sarcasm* was enlightening; coaches began to realize its adverse effects. Finally, they noted a clear correlation between the decrease in positive interactions and the increase in discipline issues across the grade levels.

After this work, the school coaches led the teachers through a similar process, replicating steps 1 and 2. In addition, the coaches included some of the following activities with the teacher groups:

- They showed video examples from classrooms or observed in various grade levels.
- They conducted the role-playing practice of giving effective feedback (*use teacher role-play*), and they debriefed afterward.
- Using *ask reflective questions*, they addressed the following: "Is this shift to positive recognition difficult?" and "How do student reactions vary by grade level?"

- Using *teach prosocial skills*, they developed anchor charts for teachers and students that listed positive interaction steps.

One unexpected outcome was that teachers decided to replicate some of the steps the coaches used with them directly with their students. Coaching social-emotional learning from data and as a team proves pivotal for teacher change.

Getting Off the Rolling Chair

Focus Strategy:

- Simply say it

Tamarra worked with a primary school coach in Los Angeles who attempted to model for a teacher the importance of using physical proximity with students when they worked in centers. The teacher's take on teaching and building relationships was sitting in a rolling vinyl office chair during the entire class, yelling across the room to students, never meeting them at eye level. Finally, the coach got on their knees, pleading, "Mrs. D., come over here, to the floor, so we can see what the students are making!" For more than 40 minutes on two separate days, the coach tried to nudge the teacher to join them with the students. The teacher didn't budge, stayed on her chair without hearing the students well, attempted to play with the students from a distance, and observed students from afar.

Exasperated, the coach asked Tamarra, "What do I do? I've tried everything. I shared an article about the importance of proximity. I modeled what to do. Nothing worked." Tamarra asked if the teacher needed the chair for a medical condition, and the coach said no. Schooled in the tactic of *simply say it,* Tamarra inquired, "Did you tell the teacher that she needed to get out of the chair, get on the floor, and get close to show care and appreciation for the students?"

The coach replied, "Well, not exactly; I mean, I was pretty obvious crawling all over the place. How could she not know?"

"Tell her directly and nicely to move out of the chair," Tamarra responded.

In the next month's visit, the coach reported that the teacher had moved to the floor. The coach admitted, "I just thought I was *so* clear, and I wasn't! She just moved. No argument. No comment. I said it nicely and with a smile. And she hasn't been back to the chair since!" Most often, we find that being explicit is more helpful to the teacher than being indirect.

They're Still in the Shrink-Wrap

 Focus Strategy:

- Start small

Keith worked with a curriculum coach and principal in Wisconsin to help a teacher who struggled with classroom management. The entire school had attended a three-day training course on a popular classroom management program involving relationship building and tactics for teaching social-emotional expectations. Each teacher had received a library of program resources for their classroom, and the school had embraced the approach—except for that one teacher, who had not fulfilled the initiative. The coach and principal requested that Keith model a discussion with the teacher.

During the session, Keith brought up the lack of data regarding program implementation. It wasn't what the kids needed, the teacher explained: "They really need more structure and firmer consequences. This won't work with our population of students." When Keith probed, asking which strategy the teacher might have considered using, the teacher responded, "I was *thinking about* the morning meeting, but because of the schedule and so much testing, I haven't been able to get to it yet. That's the one I wanted to try." Keith noticed that the teacher's resource library for the program was still in the shipping shrink-wrap, so he immediately switched to the approach *start small*.

He proposed the teacher unpack the materials "just to make sure you have everything that was supposed to be sent last fall." The teacher agreed. In opening the program for the first time, the teacher noticed a small text that might align with an upcoming literacy unit. Then the teacher and Keith spent the remainder of the coaching time planning how to use the text, as well as a few other program components for the following week. Sure enough, within a few weeks of modest work on two strategies from the program, the curriculum coach noticed tiny improvements in the teacher's classroom management and the students' social skills.

Crying on the Floor Opens the Door

 Focus Strategies:
- Teach student self-regulation
- Multiply the management bag of tricks
- Go for short-term wins

In a California school that served a marginalized community and that had persistently low student performance, a new coach encountered a transitional kindergarten teacher who artfully dodged any attempt at working with them. Tamarra and the coach observed in the classroom several times. It was clear the teacher needed help because students were continually disengaged in learning throughout the day. Students had frequent emotional outbursts. The teaching was unrelated to age-level expectations, and there was no in-class attention to the students' social or emotional needs. When the coach tried to talk to the teacher about the observations, the teacher missed the meetings, didn't reply to emails or texts, and selected a seat as far away from the coach as possible in group settings.

One afternoon, the coach and Tamarra entered the room to observe a literacy lesson. The teacher stood, straddling a screaming student crying on the floor, and repeatedly yelled at the student, "Look what you've done now! Look what you've done now!" The rest of the class started to pop out of their seats and wander around the room. After the teacher requested they call for the assistant principal, the coach asked for the opportunity to calm the student down. "That would be great," the teacher snapped, returning to the other students and moving on with the literacy lesson.

Meanwhile, the coach tried a few techniques for calming a distressed student without touching them, and the approach worked—like magic. In about three minutes (Tamarra timed it!), the student stopped yelling, stood up, and went back to their desk. According to the coach, this intervention was a bit of a record breaker in terms of time. Tamarra and the coach stayed for another 20 minutes to ensure the student remained on task and calm.

After school, the teacher stopped by the coach's office to briefly thank the coach and then quickly turned to leave. The coach jumped up and darted after them, asking the teacher if they would like to hear about the two or three processes they typically use to calm a student in distress and, specifically, what they did with that young student on the floor (basically, a couple of the tactics from *teach student self-regulation*). The coach offered to come into the class and demonstrate whole-group work on social-emotional skill building. The teacher took the offer. This work developed into a two-year process of coaching the teacher around both academic and social-emotional content.

The coach employed several strategies with this teacher:

- They increased the teacher's repertoire of strategies for social-emotional instruction with *multiply the management bag of tricks.*
- They used their Pied Piper–like strength at managing students and modeled *teach student self-regulation.*
- Finally, they borrowed a tactic from the next chapter, *go for short-term wins.*

These strategies modeled best practice and gained a receptiveness from the teacher regarding feedback and the entire coaching process.

Coaches, Consider This...

- For the teachers you work with, what are their most significant needs around social and emotional instruction?
- What strategies from this chapter can you use immediately to help teachers strengthen their relationships with students?
- What strategies from this chapter might help clarify the meaning of and need for social and emotional instruction for teachers?

5

Coaching Openness to Feedback

Remarkable educators take criticism well, make rapid and frequent changes to their classroom tactics, and are highly reflective. Openness to feedback is about how teachers comprehend what they hear in coaching—and if they act on it. Further, research findings indicate that individuals who are receptive to and solicitous of critical feedback are associated with higher performance ratings (Ashford & Tsui, 1991; Chen et al., 2007) and are more creative (Ashford & Tsui, 1991; Shalley et al., 2015). Conversely, coaches struggle when teachers are not open to feedback or engage in minimal reflection.

Hattie (2012) noted that influential teachers seek input from their students regularly; they're open to the fact that they may need to change their instruction in the moment, and they seek insights, especially from students. Kim and colleagues (2019) found that transparency, openness, and curiosity were indicative of highly skilled teachers and that effective teachers engage socially—a trait needed for one-on-one work with a coach. What's more, Costa and colleagues (2016) named *adaptability in accepting input* and *making changes* as essential prerequisites for motivated teachers. Just as those who study music or perfect their athletic game are receptive to criticism from their teachers or coaches, so too is the outstanding teacher. Experienced, professional symphonies use conductors to signal expression, cue decrescendos, and encourage sections to play more loudly; these professional musicians display an openness to feedback, judgment, and advice.

The following strategies solicit an openness to or an acceptance of feedback and promote reflective practice. Comb through them to find what you need.

Researcher	Effective Teacher Traits or Dispositions Related to Openness to Feedback
Costa et al. (2016)	• Efficacy: seeks competence, learning, self-improvement • Flexibility: sees other perspectives, adapts, changes • Consciousness: monitors and reflects on thoughts and actions of self and others
Kim et al. (2019)	• Extraversion: sociable • Openness: embraces new ideas and experiences, intellectually curious

Strategies

5.1: Start Small

Start small to facilitate more openness to coaching. Instead of trying to tackle the broader reflection—"How do you think the lesson went?"—narrow the scope of reflection by asking, "What would you change about the formative assessment?" or "What did you notice about the writing in the lab summaries?"

Teachers who possess a broad skill set in teaching and who are highly reflective will be able to analyze and correct themselves if pointed in the appropriate direction. Also, including words like *rewind, redo, tweak,* or *touch up* connotes that although the teacher *does* need to change something, they don't need to overhaul the entire lesson. All professionals and technicians are compilations of small skills built over time. To see how to structure a coaching dialogue focused on a small reflection as opposed to major reflection areas, see Figure 8.1 (pp. 224–225).

Here's a specific *start small* approach involving student and teacher interactions. First, ask the teacher to focus on an interaction with a student or class. Then analyze it using these steps:

1. **Identify.** "What did you see as effective and less effective in this interaction or discussion?"

2. **Acknowledge.** State what you, the coach, saw happening in the exchange: "I noticed that no students connected their attempted math solutions to the mathematical concept." "After a lengthy group discussion about whether the imagery in the poem stanza was feminine or masculine, you didn't ask the students what it was in the end; you simply told them it was feminine. You said, _____."

3. **Ask.** "What effect does this interaction have on students' behavior and learning?"

4. **Enhance.** Work with the teacher to plan how they will improve this interaction for next time.

5.2: Acknowledge, Acknowledge, Acknowledge

An essential characteristic of adult learners is their appreciation of their experiences (Knowles et al., 2020). A powerful way for a coach to address this need is to thoroughly acknowledge the teacher's unique background or context (Aguilar, 2013; Saphier et al., 2018). Validating a teacher's perspective smooths the way for engagement in coaching. We can't emphasize this point enough: verbally acknowledge their issues, elaborate on the details they provide, and summarize their comments. Tell them when you understand their point of view, and explain why.

5.3: Simply Say It

Simply tell the teacher what you want to see in terms of their receptivity to input: "I know you're open to feedback." "I'm sure you like to learn new things." "The most effective teachers I work with love feedback; they even solicit feedback." Use these comments or find your own words to tell them that they need to be more receptive, open-hearted, and available to the coaching process.

5.4: Give More Frequent Feedback

Suppose a teacher is unaccustomed to corrective feedback or previously encountered a bad experience with coaching. In that case, it's possible that increasing your frequency of feedback (along with showing that you're trustworthy) will create more responsiveness to coaching.

5.5: Provide Critical Feedback

Whether you call it *notes, critique, judgment, critical friend, cool and warm feedback, directional feedback,* or *instructional feedback,* provide essential, critical feedback. Research shows that people desire frank, well-supported feedback (Anderson, 2014; Fishbach & Finkelstein, 2020; Fishbach et al., 2010; Fong et al., 2018; Killion, 2019; Zenger & Folkman, 2014). Don't disparage, overwhelm, or neglect praise; deliver the appropriate critique. Some coaches think that frank, critical feedback may demotivate teachers. However, a meta-analysis of 78 studies that compared negative feedback to neutral or no feedback revealed no effect of the former on intrinsic motivation (Fong et al., 2018). The same study found that critical feedback that *motivated* individuals shared these qualities:

- The negative feedback included teaching about how to improve. The critic provided models, examples, or steps for improvement. Thus, the person receiving the critical analysis knew the precise steps necessary for change.
- The critique included a predetermined standard or criterion. It relied on an objective rubric, a standard of performance, a checklist, or another guideline to justify the negative feedback.
- The critical feedback occurred in person, not via email, a note, or a third party.

The meta-analysis from Fong and colleagues (2018) referenced several studies from Hattie's research on feedback (Hattie & Clarke, 2019). No hint in this research indicates that adults are too fragile to discuss a mistake without becoming devastated (Harmin & Toth, 2006). Deliver crucial analysis in person and from a place of professional care; base it on clear criteria and data, and include explicit information about how to improve. The more precise and detailed your script of the classroom observation, the more productive your feedback will be. Maintaining an explicit script keeps the coach from relying on what they may *think*, as opposed to what actually happened in the classroom. See example scripts in Appendix B.

Some critics of this approach claim that it's best to get the teacher to identify their faults through 100 percent self-analysis. We agree that reflective practice and self-analysis in coaching are powerful. We even include questions for teacher reflective practice at the end of every chapter of this book. Some people dislike verbally reflecting with another person; they prefer to reflect privately and mentally, and they do so quite productively. Others are simply weak at self-analysis in general; they have difficulty recalling their actions, picking them apart, and connecting their behavior to other ideas or concepts. In these cases, solely applying reflective coaching is akin to using a single screwdriver to repair a car. You can do a lot of good with a screwdriver, but you can do much damage relying on a single tool. Rather, use a range of coaching techniques, from reflective practice to collaborative problem solving to instructional coaching.

Occasionally, skipping reflection is a matter of practicality. There are times when reflection works, but getting the teacher to reach an epiphany may take longer than time allows in a complex and busy school environment. In a national training we attended, one author of a popular coaching model told us that reflective coaching could resolve any teacher's problem. When a participant asked about the maximum length of time it might take, the author replied, "About two hours." We've found that most coaches and leaders don't have two hours to address every common classroom issue with a teacher. When this is the case, use approaches other than an extended, contemplative method.

5.6: Engage in Difficult Conversations

Plan a thoughtful discussion with the teacher around the issues of being receptive to feedback and the coaching relationship. Remember to use concrete data to back up your claim that the teacher is not amenable to the process. Data might include missing coaching appointments, minimal contributions during coaching, failure to implement agreements following coaching, and so on. If needed, rehearse the conversation with a valued colleague or friend beforehand.

5.7: Link Impact

When you observe teacher adaptability and its effect on students, document it and report it to the teacher. Let's say you coached a teacher to plan DOK 3 prompts (Webb, 2002, 2007) because they weren't occurring during instruction, and when you next observed the teacher, they *did* offer such prompts and you saw a positive effect on students. Point out in the next coaching session the link between the teacher's openness to planning the questions and the direct effect on students' thinking during the class.

5.8: Borrow Teacher Language

Listen to and borrow the teacher's preferred language metaphors, whether they're visual, kinesthetic, verbal, gustatory, or social (Geary, 2011). Adopt that same vocal pattern to explain the concepts you want to coach or teach. Often, the teacher will "open a door" as they talk, so use their vocabulary as your way into a topic. Note a physical or kinesthetic preference when you hear comments such as these: "I did that because it just felt right." "It hit me in the gut when the students didn't understand what I was talking about." "It was touching when you noticed how hard I tried." "I don't have a feel for how to do this the way you described." All those touch-and-feel words are your cue to use tactile vernacular in your feedback language. Sometimes, this enables the teacher to hear and implement your critiques more readily. "Stealing Language," an implementation story at the end of this chapter, illustrates this process.

5.9: Propose a Book or Resource Study

Get a copy of *Thanks for the Feedback* (Stone & Heen, 2014), and do a thorough book study with the teacher on this exceptional, research-based text, which details all about being open to feedback. Alternatively, just pick up a copy and dive in for your own personal professional development.

5.10: Teach How to Take Feedback

Some people never learned to accept input as a regular part of professional (or personal) life. Collected here are suggestions from hundreds of coaches across the United States about assisting teachers in taking critical feedback. Teachers should

- Pretend this feedback is for someone else and that their job is to explain it to them. They'll need to listen carefully, respectfully clarify, summarize, and ask for examples and alternative solutions.

- Listen to criticism for what is true (Stone & Heen, 2014). Even if the teacher disagrees with most of a coach's critique, they may find a kernel of validity in the comments.

- Respond to feedback with "How might I do that?" or "Can you give me an example?" instead of "That's not possible."

- Approach feedback with curiosity instead of defensiveness.

- Borrow the "Yes, and…" approach from improvisational acting. The teacher should accept the critique and add to it. For example, suppose the coach recommends adding small-group instruction. Instead of defending their lack of small groups, the teacher might respond, "Yes, and how can I get that into my 45-minute lesson?" or "Yes, and what ideas do you have for work tasks in those groups?"

- Separate the feedback from the speaker. They may not like or trust the coach, but that doesn't mean the coach's input is incorrect. They should try to quiet that defensive voice and listen carefully to the coach's remarks. They should also be aware of their personal biases about religious beliefs, political views, dress, or sexual identity. Is one of these prejudices preventing them from fully receiving the coaching feedback?

- Consider patterns. Has the teacher heard something similar from someone else, even in a nonwork environment? If they're getting the same feedback from different people or places, it's information worth considering.

- Take notes. Sometimes, writing notes helps us focus on what's said, remain in the moment, and think about the content. For example, if the teacher doesn't like the input, just looking at their paper and taking extra time to write might give them a few seconds to relax and think before reacting to the critique verbally.

5.11: Manage Disagreeable Feedback

At times, the feedback may be utterly unacceptable to the teacher. Let the teacher know of actions at their disposal if they genuinely disagree with the input. As the coach, you can do the following:

- Offer a second opinion. If the resources are available, suggest that another coach or an administrator observe in the classroom to assess the same issue. Afterward, compare that feedback to yours in the session with the teacher.
- Suggest the teacher record themselves and self-analyze using the same criteria you used.
- Teach them to press for specificity (Stone & Heen, 2014). For example, tell the teacher to ask for additional examples, a different description or analogy, or a more detailed narration of what the desired result would look like in their context.
- Teach the teacher not to generalize. Let the teacher know that just because this feedback is not what they desired, *it doesn't mean* they're a terrible teacher, *it doesn't mean* they won't improve on the practice, *it doesn't mean* you don't like them, and *it doesn't mean* they'll feel this badly in the future. Most likely, the critical feedback doesn't mean any of those negative conclusions they may be attempting to associate with

the information (Gilbert, 2007; Stone & Heen, 2014). Help the teacher keep the critique in perspective.

- If another person is available, see if you can get the teacher a different coach.

5.12: Alert the Teacher to Listening Filters

Teach about filters and the significance of paraphrasing. Everything the coach says goes through the output filters of their experiences, beliefs, language styles, and education. Likewise, the teacher being coached receives the feedback through their own unique input filters. Without paraphrasing or clarification, you may not know for certain that you both have the same concept in mind.

5.13: Model How to Take Feedback

After a couple coaching sessions, model taking feedback by requesting that the teacher give *you* feedback on your coaching. Model listening, asking questions, and reflecting. This approach helps you demonstrate that feedback is good, regardless of expertise or job position. Describe how each of you approaches coaching conversations; put your descriptions into separate boxes, so to speak. Then step outside the boxes and discuss how each of you thinks and reacts to coaching feedback.

5.14: Affirm the Power of Coaching

Let the teacher know that you provide feedback to all teachers, even highly experienced or skilled teachers. If it's true, tell the teacher that you receive critical feedback from your boss and that your boss receives observation and critical feedback from their supervisor.

Remind the teacher that the goal of coaching is not to override the teacher's judgment or personality; rather, it's what a high-quality coach brings to the conversation (Stone & Heen, 2014). Ideally, your job is to help make wise, third-party judgments about what might work for the teacher's personality and skills, the needs of the students, the context of the school, and the demands of the curriculum and standards. You're there to help the teacher get best practices in place for their students, given all the complex and unique teaching factors at play in the teacher's context.

5.15: Reference Analogies

Frame teacher coaching from an athletic coach or a music teacher. Just as a softball coach continually critiques how an athlete places their feet when up at bat or a cello teacher makes learners replay music sections regardless of their age or experience, a teacher coach provides similar feedback. Over the course of a lifetime, many adults become engaged in some venture where they received precise, critical feedback. Gather analogies and metaphors that help communicate the essential nature of feedback in everyday life (Geary, 2011).

5.16: Display Open Body Language

Ensure you're physically reflecting that you're mentally and emotionally ready to hear what the teacher communicates. Lean slightly forward, make generous eye contact, and uncross your arms and hands (Grant et al., 2018). Ask a colleague to check your take on open body language and get their frank opinion. Coach peer reviews often noted unconscious behaviors like playing with jewelry or mindlessly twirling a pen. These actions may lead a person to think that you're not fully listening to them.

5.17: Ask Reflective Questions

To strengthen and solicit thinking about openness and receptivity during coaching, ask one or more of the following questions:

- What would you improve about our coaching meetings?
- How do you think we could focus more on student outcomes during our time together?
- You mentioned my suggestions for the last lesson were helpful. What made you more receptive to the ideas?
- How might your issues about criticism be getting in your way?
- How are you showing up with your best self (or your full self) in this coaching process?
- How are you becoming more receptive to critical feedback?
- Are you open to new ideas? Give me some examples.
- How could you improve your listening skills?
- How are your past experiences with feedback shaping our work together?
- What do we need to do to keep you receptive to critical feedback?

5.18: Share Your Lack of Experience

Sometimes a teacher may say, "How can you advise me? You've never taught _____ or had _____ kind of student." In this situation, bring up the issues of experience and expertise in the coaching relationship. For example, you might say, "You know, I've never taught AP chemistry; however, I've taught high school math for nine years, and I do know what it's like to implement new standards or a new program" or "Even athletes at the highest level in their sport receive expert coaching from others who never played at their level; sometimes they have several coaches." Then explain the coach's significance as the objective eye in the classroom and as a professional brainstorming partner. There will likely always be a new curriculum, assessment, or program you have no experience with. When you can, get practice with it: teach a summer class, help administer the new assessment, or coteach the subject. When you can't gain some experience, learn as much as you can about the topic, stay humble, and stay focused on the purpose of your role.

5.19: Work on Your Relationship Skills

Here are some tips for how coaches can improve relationships with the adults they serve:

- Even if you're not highly extroverted, be curious about working with and learning from new people. Remember details about the teachers—their hobbies, families, and quirks. Try to learn one new professional or personal detail about a person each time you talk with them. These details help build the partnership and may help you form analogies that facilitate their learning.

- Pay attention to bids for connection—a subtle nod, a look, a question, a smile, or an utterance of "hmmm" while reading or looking at something. These expressions call for an emotional connection (Gottman & Silver, 2015). Pay attention and engage. Ask, "What's so funny (or interesting)?" or "What's on your mind?" Start listening for those little calls for attention, and you'll notice they occur more frequently than you realize.

- Avoid oversharing. Remember, the coaching relationship's focus is on improving the teacher's professional capacity and student experiences. We surveyed a few hundred coaches internationally about this issue, and they recommended that coaches could share the following:
    » Your teaching and education experiences.

» Your general marital or parenting status.
» Your experience being coached.
» Your philosophy of education.
» Your personal beliefs about student learning.
» Your experience learning and failing or stumbling to learn new things.

Conversely, you shouldn't share the following information:

» Complaints about your boss.
» Conversations from others you coach.
» Your political affiliation and politics in general. Several coaches share nothing about politics, whereas some said that general information, like party affiliation, was fine.
» Your marital or relationship issues.
» Parenting problems with your children.
» Details about your personal health.
» Religious views. Several coaches never broach the topic of religion, whereas some in heavily religious communities said sharing information about sect or denominational status was OK.

Leaders also provided insight regarding another circumstance—when they're the only person representing a marginalized population in their setting. Some coaches from disenfranchised populations felt like ambassadors for the communities they represented, and they gladly shared details about their population or facts that teachers were unaware of or that were pertinent to coaching issues. On the other hand, some coaches in that same situation believed the responsibility for learning about marginalized groups rested primarily with the majority population; it wasn't their responsibility to be the sole source of information about their community. Coaches need not assume they're the primary source of information about a population. Share as you prefer and provide readings and other resources as the need arises. Let teachers know they may need to do homework on their own regarding the topic.

5.20: Be Friendly—But Not Necessarily a Friend

Occasionally, a coach admits that they're trying to be friends with the staff they coach because they learned that trust and rapport are crucial aspects of coaching. Although we agree that reliability and connectedness are significant to the professional relationship, making everyone your friend will prove untenable.

Instead, try this. Consider people you trust and connect with in your life but who are not friends, relatives, or colleagues. When we ask this question in workshops, blank stares greet us. "I've got nobody," someone offers. Then, after some wait time and a bit of group discussion, people start naming their accountant, their physician, a soccer coach, a college mentor, the veterinarian, their mechanic, and so on. Consider how such people gained your trust and rapport without becoming close friends. We first encountered an activity similar to this in a workshop by Laurie Crehan in Frankfurt, Germany. Later, a version of it appeared in *Blended Coaching* (Bloom et al., 2005).

Once you hold a clear vision of how you want to show up in the coaching relationship, use it as a screen or filter for your behaviors. Suppose you're wondering whether you should purchase a holiday gift for the teacher you coach or pick up coffee and donuts for them on the way to work. Ask yourself, "Would I do this for my mechanic or the family doctor?" If the answer is yes, then by all means, go for it. For most coaches, the response is no. Your image of the partnership helps you reflect on your motivations and the actions you need to take to maintain and grow the relationship appropriately for the work environment.

5.21: Be Cautious About Offering Non-Work-Related Advice

Because of the intensity of the relationship and your skills at building trust and rapport, sometimes teachers ask for personal advice unrelated to, or peripherally related to, their teaching work. We suggest a great deal of caution here. However, a few approaches we have deployed or seen other coaches use can help manage this scenario:

- Acknowledge the issue. Say, "That must be tough; I can't imagine how challenging that can be." You don't need to problem solve or assume responsibility for every topic a teacher brings up. Be sincere, be human, and just rest with the challenge presented. Take some deep breaths or pause before commenting, "I know that topic is weighing heavily on your mind right now, but I'm going to gently move us on to our next issue."
- Be prepared with resources. Have contact information for the human resources department or local community organizations. Try "That's not my area of expertise, but here's contact information for others in our system" or "There are people way more qualified than me to talk to about this." One coach worked with teachers who primarily spoke Arabic but who worked in an English-speaking community. Ready with potential referrals, the coach kept a stack of business cards for Arabic-speaking attorneys, accountants, social workers, therapists, food banks, and others.
- Set clear expectations and parameters for the coaching discussion at the beginning of the relationship (Grant et al., 2018). Then, when topics arise outside that domain, gently remind the teacher of the norms you both established early on. For example, say, "I really do wish we could explore this

issue; I can feel how important it is to you. Part of my job is to protect our time together and those agreements we set early on. For this reason, we're going to need to respectfully move that subject off the table and focus on our teaching and learning issues."

- If the teacher appears emotionally overwhelmed and unable to focus due to an issue unrelated to coaching, ask if they need to take a short break or to reschedule the session.

5.22: Focus on Practical Feedback

Analyze the issues you see and focus the coaching conversation on actual problems for the teacher or students. Anytime you can tie coaching to student outcomes, do so. If you're unsure if your approach is practical, then work with a colleague, a lead teacher, or an administrator and conduct joint observations, calibrate your critiques, and ensure you're leading the teacher with valuable recommendations. One of the primary characteristics of adult learners is that they like their learning to solve practical problems (Knowles et al., 2020). For more on adult learner characteristics, see Chapter 7.

5.23: Go for Short-Term Wins

Occasionally, a teacher may be exceptionally unreceptive to feedback. They might miss appointments, avoid talking to you, or stop teaching when you enter the classroom. Observe them a few times, try to engage them in conversations about issues they encounter, and see if you can solve an urgent problem for them. Maybe they need supplemental curriculum materials, which you can get from the district office. Perhaps they have a particularly challenging student, and you know quick strategies for getting that student on task. Offer this help early on.

These short-term wins are often a way to open the relationship to coaching and receiving critical feedback. We've even heard a coach say, "You know, I went out on a limb to get you that extra set of novels. Now I need a favor in return: I need you to complete a couple rounds of coaching with me." Of course, it's not the coach's primary job to be the supply clerk or behavior specialist for the teacher in the long term. Still, at the beginning of the relationship, these actions may add credibility and build rapport and help the coaching work move forward.

5.24: Switch Settings

Pay attention to the teacher's needs. Do they need to sit because they've been on their feet all day? Do they need to get fresh air by walking and talking with you outside? Do they need to eat lunch or have a snack while chatting? Would they rather meet in your office or their classroom? Sometimes just suggesting a change in the environment provides enough motivation to get the person talking. For example, one coach in upstate New York proved popular with staff because they often took teachers on a "coach walk and talk" around a massive baseball field adjacent to the school. We refer to this approach as *ramble coach* (Matheson, 2019); see it and other approaches in Chapter 8.

If there's a significant difference in size or height between the coach and teacher, consider sitting down to talk. Sitting, as opposed to standing, deemphasizes both parties' size and potential power differential, placing both closer to eye level. One coach in San Francisco who stood two feet shorter than any other adult in the building conducted all their coaching from an adjustable-height, rolling office chair. This way, they could quickly adjust the chair height to work with the teacher at eye level.

5.25: Build Trust

Lack of trust may lead to a lack of openness; work to gain teacher trust. Trust is typically learned over time. All the same, there are a few quick and simple ways to gain it. We collected several tactics over the years and adapted approaches outlined by several authors (Aguilar, 2013, 2016; Bloom et al., 2005; Knight, 2016). Review this list and do a self-check to see what you should start or stop doing:

- Share your goal for coaching with the teacher, your intent behind the conversations. Be explicit about what you will and won't discuss and with whom you'll share the information. Don't break your promise.
- Keep your word about time commitments, offering resources, and so on. In general, guarantee less and overdeliver.
- Be aware that just because a classroom strategy worked for you and 87 other teachers, that doesn't mean it will work this time with this teacher or that student.
- Demonstrate basic politeness and personal interest. Share personal information if it helps the teacher move forward in their practice, but make sure your coaching relationship is more about making an exceptional teacher than making a new friend.
- Be quick to admit mistakes, and state what you don't know. You can't know everything about all aspects of schooling.
- At the same time, study up. Learn a new curriculum, and practice teaching it. Instruct a course or small group of students regularly. Read widely and attend training; stay current with the research and contemporary curriculum, instruction, and assessment practices. Several high school department chairs we work with teach one course while coaching or supervising teachers; this keeps them grounded in the day-to-day work of teaching. Some elementary school coaches take on a small

intervention group for mathematics or reading to provide academic student support and sharpen their teaching skills.

- Above all, be consistent. This consistency of character and the quality of your feedback most often predict whether teachers will or won't gain trust in you.

5.26: Offer Think Time

If the teacher is not responding to the coaching conversation, give them time to absorb what they heard. Some people are overwhelmed by critical feedback. Occasionally, people need to mull over the information before effectively problem solving or verbally reflecting on what they've heard. You might say something like this: "Let's hit the pause button. Take a day to think about this feedback, and then we'll meet to work through it and make a plan of action." Providing wait time helps engage more quiet learners (Grant et al., 2018).

5.27: Ask More *What* Than *Why* Questions

For some people, asking *why* can be a trigger, and *why* questions often mask recommendations we're trying to make as a coach. We might ask, "*Why* did you wait until the last two minutes of the school day to pack up and line up 28 6-year-olds?" when our actual thought was "That was an unreasonable expectation for an end-of-day transition."

To avoid the *why*, try switching to *what*. Instead, you might ask, "What was going through your mind with that 2-minute closing transition?" Instead of "Why did you respond that way?" try, "What response were you expecting from the student when you said _____?" Instead of "Why did you go off the curriculum," try, "What thoughts prompted you to switch from the curriculum guide?"

The *what* questions are more likely to get at the motivation for the teacher's actions, while leaving them receptive to ideas for solving problems you observed. Put the prompt in Figure 5.1 at the top of your coaching notes as a reminder of this shift; do this, and you just made yourself a job aid.

Figure 5.1   Shift from "Why" to "What" Questions

5.28: Create Brave Spaces

During coaching, let teachers speak their truth without ridiculing them. Occasionally, a teacher may make a statement you find offensive or antithetical to student learning, such as "Some kids just don't want to learn; it is not my job to force them." Remember that what is said is data for you to use as a coach to help this teacher become a better teacher. You may not be prepared to respond immediately. Keep in mind that you do not need to agree or show approval; you can simply move on and know that you will need to find a way to change this attitude as you work with them. Make speaking candidly and respectfully a norm that you revisit at the beginning and end of every session. Do this until it's a common practice. Provide discussion or listening protocols for talking about potentially sensitive topics. The story "Success Opens a Door" at the end of this chapter illustrates this process. For more ideas about brave spaces, see the work of Murphey and D'Auria (2021).

5.29: Establish Clear Goals

The coaching process should maintain clear objectives or targets to reach and celebrate. Does the school need urgent instructional practices? Does the teacher need to become proficient in a conceptual approach to teaching language arts? Is it clear what curriculum fidelity looks like? Be precise about teacher expectations and how those expectations are measured through the coaching process; communicate this to the teacher repeatedly. The coach may provide a clear checklist of curriculum components that reveals teacher implementation or progress on implementation as indicated through coach observations.

5.30: Present Awards in Front of Students

Provide positive feedback or awards in front of students rather than in front of other teachers. For example, interrupt the classroom (with permission from the teacher) and present the teacher with a certificate or flowers and explain why you're doing that. What has the teacher done to increase learning? Always base the awards on teaching and learning protocols or goals that teachers know. This is one of the most palatable types of recognition we've seen for teachers, and this type of award for reaching coaching goals may inspire more engagement in the coaching process.

5.31: Role-Play Reflection

With the teacher you're coaching, watch a video of a different teacher teaching. First, ask the teacher to assume the role of the teacher appearing in the video. Then have them reflect on how the teaching went in that example as though *they* had taught the lesson. Sometimes, having the teacher step outside themselves to reflect helps them take feedback less personally and become more critical of themselves.

5.32: Observe Another Teacher Reflect

Take the teacher you're coaching to another teacher's coaching debrief—a teacher who is a skilled reflector. Afterward, discuss with the teacher what they heard. Give the observing teacher a note-taking guide if you think it will help them focus on what they're hearing and on what might be missing in their own reflective practice. We're often delighted by how surprised some teachers are when they hear a colleague engaging in detailed self-critique.

5.33: Promote Self-Coaching

Record a lesson of the teacher teaching, and let the teacher self-coach on the basis of what they see in the video. Have them do this next to you. Again, this strategy may help the teacher depersonalize feedback and relax a bit more into a thoughtful review of their teaching performance with a coach.

5.34: Journal First, Talk Second

Sometimes people are more reflective if they write first. Ask the teacher to keep a reflective journal. Suggest, "At the end of the day or lesson, jot down two things you would change and two things you would keep doing." Getting them to break down reflection into smaller chunks of time and writing down their thoughts instead of talking may promote more self-analysis. We attribute this idea to Vickie Lake, associate dean at the University of Oklahoma. Lake uses this process when teaching controversial topics to doctoral students.

5.35: Take a Strength-Based Stance

To accelerate reflection, we turn to positive psychology (Seligman & Csikszentmihalyi, 2014). Start by focusing on the teacher's strengths and have them analyze their practice from there; highlight what they performed with ease and excellence (Buckingham & Goodall, 2019; Dumbro et al., 2020). Next, analyze with them why this practice worked so well. Then plan to apply similar principles to an issue that needs improvement. Once they're accustomed to self-critiques and getting into a flow of excellence, they may opt to examine all aspects of their practice, not solely their strengths.

Another version of this strategy is to coach the teacher's strengths and disregard critical feedback—for a brief period. In Chapter 8, you'll find our Positive Descriptive Appreciation app, which we use to structure positive feedback. See if this approach helps the teacher open up to positive or neutral feedback. Then start placing tiny bits of critical feedback into the coaching conversations.

5.36: Push Curiosity and Awareness

Work to kindle interest and imagination in the teacher. The heart of mindfulness, which is closely associated with reflection, is curiosity and awareness (Brewer, 2017). Try prompting curiosity with a few of these prompts:

- I wonder what would happen if _____.
- Who's holding you back from trying that idea?
- Let's pretend your students could do this thinking if they had the foundational skills. What kind of lesson would that look like? In the meantime, what kind of support could you toss in to help them with missing foundations while they work at the higher-level thinking skills?
- If time constraints were not an issue, what might you do differently?
- What awareness are you taking away from this coaching session?
- Let's take that student out of the equation. Let's plan as if they'll be absent that day. What will you do in this scenario?

- Let's just brainstorm some ideas. Toss out anything without giving it too much judgment.
- What are some exciting next steps? What are you inspired to do?

5.37: Avoid Vague Recommendations and Generalized Praise

Be specific with recommendations. Try not to say things such as "You need to be more aware" or "You're super-innovative." We sometimes see a lack of openness or receptivity because our advice is too vague. It's far more effective to provide the steps or actions that *determine* awareness or the precise moves that made you call out innovation. For example, instead of saying, "You need to be more assertive," you might say, "When giving directions, you need to stand still, turn your body to face the majority of students, look students in the eye, and phrase your requests as clear expectations, not questions."

5.38: Engage in Collaborative Group Feedback

Ask a team of teachers to plan a lesson together, then have them watch one another implement that lesson. Encourage them all to focus on the students. After they watch one another teach, ask them to regroup to talk about something they observed that positively affected student learning (providing evidence for their claim) and something they observed that could be more effective (again, providing evidence). When teachers see giving and receiving feedback as a reciprocal event, feedback becomes part of the culture. As a coach, provide them with input on the way they give one another feedback. Ask all participants to share the feedback they found most important and explain why. Keep the focus on the effect on student learning.

This approach works incredibly well if you begin with a group willing to be a "fishbowl" for others. In this instance, one team, grade level, or department conducts a round of collaborative group feedback while another team sits to the side, observes, and takes notes. This gives the observing group a live example of the process.

5.39: Ditch the Sandwich; Number the Steps

We'd like to point out a couple of coaching approaches to avoid. These include "two glows and a grow" and the "feedback sandwich" advocated by the pseudoscientific practices of neurolinguistic programming (James & Shephard, 2001). Several researchers and authors point out the disadvantage of the feedback sandwich model, primarily because it buries and loses the main focus of the critique (Clark, 2013; Killion, 2019; Von Bergen et al., 2014).

If you're looking for a formula or simple outline for the coaching conversation, we suggest numbering the steps. At the beginning of our work training principals and coaches, several struggled to demonstrate a focused, comprehensible coaching conversation. We would explain, model, watch, present, and model repeatedly, with minimal progress in some cases. Then we added numbered steps to the process and witnessed leaders' coaching proficiently sail forward.

In Chapter 8, you'll find our four coaching apps: the Positive Descriptive Appreciation (PDA) app, the Mini-Reflect app (for minor issues), the Major-Reflect app (for highly reflective teachers), and the Instruct app (for significant missed opportunities). The focus of each differs somewhat in the beginning, middle, and end of a coaching conversation. For example, in the Instruct app, at the beginning of the conversation, you would state the student's missed opportunity; in the middle, you would teach the practice needed; and at the end, you would set a time to see the teacher implementing the new practice.

Some principals literally place the steps beside their coaching notes and discreetly glance at them from time to time throughout the coaching session to keep themselves on track as they learn the process. Some coaches disclose their learning to the teacher, pointing out, "Oh, wait. I'm learning a new coaching process. Let me look at my outline and see if I hit all the steps I planned. Oh! I need you to summarize; I almost forgot that part!" This transparency enables the teacher to see their leader as a learner as well.

5.40: Make the Conversation Physically Active

If the teacher moves like molasses to make changes, consider taking more active approaches during the coaching conversation. We've recommended role-playing, scripting, and planning during coaching chats, and these ideas work. Consider adding any other reasonable action that causes the teacher to inch toward production. Take the upcoming student practice problems and rewrite them, ask the teacher to take notes, sort student work bins, arrange furniture and other provisions for the lesson, write the whiteboard configuration, or edit the digital slideshow to include improvements. Do part of the work the teacher needs to complete during the coaching conversation.

5.41: Normalize the Error

If the teacher is upset or emotional about a significant mistake they made, one that is not uncommon, help them normalize the situation. Try to move them to solve or correct the issue instead of beating themselves up. You'll want to use *acknowledge, acknowledge, acknowledge* to respect how they feel; they may need ample silence, so *offer think time*. At the same time, nudge them to see the incident as typical.

This time may be the perfect moment to *use social data (stories)*; tell a story about how you or a teacher you know made a similar mistake and how they addressed it. One coach in Norfolk, Virginia, was a pro at managing challenging student behaviors and considered a district expert in social-emotional education. That coach often told teachers about their first year in the classroom when they lost patience and screamed at a group of 6th graders, "You're acting like a bunch of *children!*" The youngest, smallest, most angelic student in the class beamed up from the front row and replied, "But we *are* children, Miss." The story helped many laugh and relax a bit when working to overcome errors in student management.

5.42: Discuss Triggers

Have a candid conversation with the teacher about the likelihood of upsetting them while coaching. Let them know you may unintentionally offend them and that you want them to talk about it if it happens. If they're triggered in that way, suggest they ask you to pause the talk; have them take some deep breaths or take a brief break, if needed. Tell them to let you know what's happening. You might even role-play this scenario early on, so it's easier for them to do it later on. Let them know you want to keep talking even if the talk is challenging, sensitive, or complex. Also, consider sharing strategies you've used in the past when someone has angered or offended you. How did you manage a microaggression and continue to communicate with the person?

Stone and Heen (2014) suggest several strategies to mitigate defensiveness or hypersensitivity. Share these as needed:

- Monitor your thinking. Pause when you start thinking thoughts such as "I wonder what this person's agenda is? What's wrong with them?" Instead, pause and think, "Is this a blind spot for me? Perhaps it's something I've never seen before?"

- Prepare for negative feedback ahead of time. Imagine yourself being calm and listening for what might be true.
- Note patterns. Mentally step back during the conversation and think, "Wow, this is where I typically go off track and start generalizing, crying, or blaming others." Pause, try to quiet that voice, and be open to more curiosity around the feedback.

What It Looks Like in Practice

Big Wins with Data

 Focus Strategies:
- Differentiate between big and little data
- Use data from others
- Go for short-term wins

Angela played a pivotal role in coaching a school turnaround in a large, marginalized urban community. She and the newly hired principal began work at the high school at the same time. Many teachers at the school didn't see a reason for change, even though scores had stagnated at a low average, the school was losing enrollment, and the staff was not open to feedback. As a result, the leadership team of administrators and teacher curriculum leaders put together a simple, two-pronged approach: (1) they conducted exit interviews with students about why they were leaving, and (2) they each selected a teacher in the building who seemed open to change and engaged them in a conversation about the school's big data and the implication they had for the future.

The students told the leaders they were leaving because "no one cared." The leadership team made a big mistake that first year; they assumed they knew what the students meant and started putting programs in place to improve the social and emotional culture of the school. A year later, when students were still leaving, the school leaders were perplexed and continued with the exit interviews, including the question, *Have the new programs made a difference?* The students were clear. They were not interested in programs to help them feel socially comfortable. That was *not* what they meant by *caring*. They meant that no one cared whether or not they *learned*. They wanted help succeeding academically. The new, more explicit information made the leadership team shift to more significant changes in their instructional systems and provide more academic support.

As for the second step—engaging staff—the teacher curriculum leaders initially communicated that leadership really cared about their jobs; teachers were concerned because fewer students meant fewer teaching positions. The leaders also emphasized how student success was essential to the school's overall success. The work of learning and change started with the lead teachers, who expressed incredible curiosity to study new methods and structures around student academic supports. That teacher leader study group grew to include more than a third of the faculty of 100 within three years. The teacher leadership team built interdisciplinary "houses" for 9th graders—smaller cohorts of teachers and students—that focused on the academic success of all students and included reinventing the curriculum, team teaching, and other initiatives.

The change grew from a group of teachers, prompted by Angela and the principal, who implemented *differentiate between big and little data* among the teacher leaders; *use data from others,* particularly from the students; and *go for short-term wins* with the first-year improvements in esprit de corps. As a result, student test scores increased, student exits decreased, and the faculty and students received state achievement accolades.

Capitalizing on Collective Efficacy

Focus Strategies:

- Differentiate between big and little data
- Acknowledge, acknowledge, acknowledge
- Teach how to take feedback
- Affirm the power of coaching

At a high school in the U.S. Southwest, the administration recognized that their big and little data matched. Both in-school and out-of-school scoring assessments revealed similar results: academic success outside of their advanced and honors programs was unacceptably low. Initially, the leaders focused on school climate, but after some consideration, the principal began a lesson-design program that brought three to five teachers in for half a day to create standards-based plans with a consultant. The teachers so enjoyed talking and learning about one another's curriculum and teaching methods that they agreed to coach one another on implementing the techniques they were learning. They followed the lead of the consultant who used *acknowledge, acknowledge, acknowledge* to signal positive points in the lesson plans before providing guidance. The teachers became willing to try new strategies. Also, the principal employed *teach how to take feedback* by critiquing one teacher who enjoyed getting feedback and who modeled a willingness to accept ideas and make them their own.

The entire faculty participated in at least one session of the lesson-design program. The assistant principal and department chairs began to facilitate the sessions themselves as the consultant coached them in *affirm the power of coaching*. Being coached and getting feedback became a campuswide norm. Scores increased among all groups of students.

Praising Teachers in Front of Students

Focus Strategy:

- Present awards in front of students

After struggling with a faculty divided by several issues over many years, a new principal and coach team decided that rewarding teachers who were adopting and adapting positive teaching strategies might encourage others. Instead, the rewards created more hostility; teachers requested there be no recognition in front of their peers. Consequently, the principal and coach decided to change the format; they adopted *present awards in front of students*.

They made certificates of excellence in each area of teaching and learning under the school's instructional focus. Then they went into classrooms and asked teachers if they could briefly address the students. The principal described what great work their teacher was doing and how dedicated they were to helping students learn; they then presented the teacher with a certificate and a small gift card (donated by alumni and the parent-teacher organization). After that, teachers could choose to tell other adults in the building about their award. Students were intrigued that their teachers were learning new strategies and that the administration valued helping teachers learn. Some teachers reported that students were more willing to try new things following the teacher in-class award presentations, and student behaviors improved.

Stealing Language

Focus Strategies:

- Borrow teacher language
- Rekindle professional motivation

Angela once coached a teacher who did not see themselves as wildly successful. However, when the teacher talked, they frequently spoke about their ability to "make things work." They gave all sorts of examples of how they could jury-rig electricity and build habitats for farm animals in a challenging space with few resources. When asked why they did this, the teacher spoke of a love for animals and the desire to help animals "beat the odds."

Angela slowly moved the conversation, using that teacher's language, into the context of the classroom. Angela described the teacher's passion for students and why many students needed a unique way to connect with the curriculum; *students needed jury-rigging to beat the odds of not succeeding academically.* Of course, the teacher already knew much of this. It was just a matter of nudging them to change their perspective (using the teacher's own terminology) and see a new way of thinking about making students successful. Adults like to solve problems using what they know. Angela relied primarily on *borrow teacher language* and *rekindle professional motivation* to get the teacher to that point.

Success Opens a Door

 Focus Strategies:

- Create brave spaces
- Engage in collaborative group feedback

After watching several classrooms of 1st graders unsuccessfully attempt academic conversations using a new protocol, Tamarra brought the teachers together and, with humor, implemented *create brave spaces.* She provided them with a safe place and time by allowing them to set the agenda and direct the work. They were allowed to be completely honest about why their students weren't following the academic conversation protocol. After many stories of frustration, the teachers stated that their students simply weren't capable of following it. It also became clear that they were all far more comfortable teaching math than teaching language arts. Tamarra suggested that they plan a lesson including academic conversations and observe one another to see if they could determine a root cause for the students' inability to follow the protocol.

After the observations, Tamarra facilitated reciprocal feedback with *engage in collaborative group feedback*. A door opened! The teachers realized that their instructions for engaging in academic conversations varied and that none were very clear. They got excited and pulled out some anchor charts they had used in math to help students follow the steps and check themselves along the way. They simply reworded the steps, including self-checks, and the student academic conversations improved significantly. Tamarra asked to sit in and watch the teachers present this new approach because the strategy might be something to use across grade levels.

Strengths-Based Stance for Off-Base Assessment

 Focus Strategy:

- Take a strength-based stance

Tamarra worked with a kindergarten teacher on an observational assessment. Most of the teacher's anecdotal data didn't match the individual assessment items, which would show student progress. The teacher's data were overwhelmingly incorrect. Tamarra would end up heavily critiquing the work during coaching, so she decided to *take a strength-based stance* during feedback.

First, Tamarra combed through the stacks of teacher observations and found the few correct examples that existed. Then, during the meeting, she and the teacher reviewed the examples and compared them to the assessment criteria. Intentionally, Tamarra reviewed the correct teacher examples first. She delivered a great deal of praise, and the teacher was feeling pretty good. Then, when they turned to the incorrect teacher samples, Tamarra started using open-ended prompts: "How does this one work, compared to the criteria?" and "Let's discuss how this one aligns with the assessment."

The teacher was shocked. "Oh my!" she exclaimed. "Why did I put this here? This just doesn't make sense!"

When the teacher asked whether those observations were "bad," Tamarra replied that they were, in fact, high-quality observational notes—it's just that they didn't match the criteria requested from the assessment. The teacher agreed and suggested they remove those observations. Tamarra then encouraged the teacher to review more examples with the same critical lens. The session went well, and the teacher embraced the critique because Tamarra had started from a solid foundation of coaching based on strengths.

Coaches, Consider This...

- Coaching "openness to feedback" is a significant issue that many coaches report. In addition to what you read in this chapter, what are other ideas you could try for gaining teacher engagement in the coaching process?
- Plan to try a few strategies from this chapter with a target teacher. What ideas do you have in mind?
- After a few weeks, return here and jot down what happened.
  » What worked? What didn't work?

  » What will you do differently moving forward with the target teacher?

6

Coaching Lesson Planning

Proficient educators are organized (Costa et al., 2016; Kim et al., 2019). They work on their technical proficiency at instruction (Costa et al., 2016; Hattie, 2012) and are frequently artistic in facilitating students' learning of a skill or concept. Successful teaching follows careful thought or planning; sometimes, teachers think about specific lessons for years. Sometimes the skill of planning doesn't occur naturally to teachers; therefore, it's incumbent on the coach to bridge the gap between ineffective and productive planning for teachers.

This chapter tackles the serious and often tedious coaching around planning—helping teachers understand the big picture in academic concepts and curriculum and translate those ideas into the precise steps of everyday teaching and learning.

Researcher	Effective Teacher Traits or Dispositions Related to Lesson Planning
Costa et al. (2016)	• Skillfulness: desires to be professionally explicit, elegant, precise
Hattie (2012)	• Monitors learning and provides feedback
Kim et al. (2019)	• Conscientiousness: highly responsible, organized, planned

Strategies

6.1: Start Small

If teachers struggle with a conceptual understanding of the standard, as well as with lesson planning and effective instructional delivery, consider starting with instructional coaching around understanding the standard or concept in the content. After that work is complete, move on to breaking down that one standard into a sequence of appropriate lessons. Finally, thoroughly plan one lesson. Breaking down multiple standards into practical lessons right at the start can prove too daunting for some teachers, especially novice or struggling teachers (NASEM, 2018).

6.2: Plan, Don't Just Improvise

Many teachers believe they can "wing" their lessons because they've done them so many times and felt successful; this attitude can be challenging to change. If you're working with an off-the-cuff teacher, ask them about their mental process as they put together a lesson. Take notes as they talk. When they're finished, walk through the components of effective planning, and ask them which ones are part of their mental process and which ones are not. Get into their mental model of planning. Ask, "What are your key reasons for not creating written plans? What might change if you did plan? What issues arise because of a lack of planning?" Listen for any mention of planning for English language learners or students with special needs. Differentiation is often left out when winging lessons.

6.3: Offer Short-Cuts

Help teachers be efficient instructional planners. Shortage of time is often the number one reason for lack of planning (Jackson, 2018). Offer simple planning outlines that enable the teacher to jot down ideas rather than write lengthy explanations and descriptions. Help them see how planning might save them time (not running to the copy machine at the last minute) and decrease their work during the lesson. See Robyn Jackson's *Never Work Harder Than Your Students and Other Principles of Great Teaching* (2018) for more constructive ideas about planning.

6.4: See Both the Big and Little Picture

Introduce the notion of *coherence* and the necessity for learning to make sense. Start in pieces, beginning with the big picture (the standards, overarching themes, thinking skills development, current performance data, and so on) and plan backward for daily objectives to ensure the coherence of the learning. An excellent resource for starting this conversation is Chapters 18 and 19 in *The Skillful Teacher* (Saphier et al., 2018). The idea is to go backward and consider the outcomes (the standard, the lesson formative assessment, and so on) *before* planning the activities that will move students to the larger pieces of learning.

Another engaging way to start planning and stay focused on student goals involves beginning with the formative assessment; precisely, how will students independently show what they learned during the lesson? Are they going to write something? Will they demonstrate something? Will they verbally respond to a question? Will they answer three key questions? How will you differentiate for dual-language learners so they can show what they have learned? With the performance firmly established, move on and write the lesson target. Continue by mapping out what the teacher will model or explore with the students, and plan examples for students to practice or work on together. Consider the language requirements of the lesson, and plan to make the content accessible for dual-language learners.

Even proficient teams can miss the mark by spending too much time on activities that don't solicit appropriate student thinking. For example, a group of 5th grade social studies teachers intended to help students understand the multicultural factors influencing life across the United States. They also wanted students to focus on state capitals because that was part of the 5th grade curriculum. Teacher 1 had students memorize all 50 states and capitals and then research and compare cultural aspects of two of their favorite states. Teacher 2 placed students in work groups to plan a road trip across the United States for visitors from another country; they were to give visitors as broad a perspective of the United States as possible while making stops in 10 state capitals. Students had to divide up the work, study the capitals, share their knowledge, justify their choices for the capitals they selected for the stops, and collaborate to plan the trip. Much of this experience involved visuals, which helped dual-language learners meet the expectations.

Comparing the two assignments, the students in Teacher 2's class not only learned about the state capitals but also developed a long-term appreciation for the diversity of culture in the United States and practiced multiple state standards and DOK 3 thinking. By contrast, although Teacher 1's approach of memorizing 50 states and capitals was challenging and time-consuming, it didn't meet the complexity of the standards or encourage higher-level thinking.

Now consider the 4th grade standard *Apply the area and perimeter formulas for rectangles in real-world and mathematical problems.* In many classrooms, the learning activity might include the following question: "What's the perimeter of a school garden that is a rectangle with two sides that are 10 feet long and two sides that are 12 feet long?" Alternatively, the teacher could take students outside for 20 minutes and ask them to work in pairs to look around the grounds and solve this problem: "I have 2"×4" boards that are 6 feet long. Each board costs $5.00. Make a plan for a border around a raised section of your chosen part of the school garden." Afterward, students must individually answer the following questions:

- Why did you choose your section of the garden?
- What is the plan for your border?
- How many boards do you need? How do you know?
- How much will it cost?
- Write a letter to your principal convincing them to accept your proposed garden border.

6.5: Observe Another Teacher Planning

To provide a model of productive teacher planning, have the teacher observe you coplanning with another teacher who is reflective about their practice and a thorough planner. Give the teacher you're coaching guided notes to take during the planning. Have the teacher direct specific questions about planning to the teacher they observe.

6.6: Count the Minutes, Literally

Ask the teacher to track, over a week or two, how much time they spend lesson planning for one class; some teachers don't know. They might time themselves using their phone, or, if they plan online, they can use one of several time-tracking apps/websites. They might respond, "I plan every Sunday afternoon." Find out exactly how long it takes them to plan for one complete lesson and whether that lesson is a 20-, 60-, or 90-minute class. Once you have a solid number, compare that to their weekly schedule and to the average time teachers spend planning a lesson, according to the research (National Council on Teacher Quality, 2012; OECD, 2014a, 2014b).

We've found that experienced teachers spend about 15–20 minutes preparing a typical class and possibly more time for more complex concepts or reteaching. New or struggling teachers often need additional time to plan. Sometimes, simply being aware of the actual time it takes instead of grousing, "There isn't enough time for planning," helps teachers repair problems budgeting their time. Also, remind new teachers that it's typical to spend more time planning during the first year or two of teaching.

6.7: Flip the Frame of Planning

Take teachers through an activity about planning focused on student learning, as opposed to planning focused on content delivery. Instead of looking at teacher action, consider what the student does, produces, thinks, calculates, defends, answers, builds, or writes. Lesson plan from the learner's perspective. Who are the students, specifically? What do they need as individuals and as a group? Create a T-chart with one side labeled "Teacher Activities" and the other side labeled "Student Activities." This visual often helps teachers *see* what students will be doing and how they will engage in the lesson. For an example of how this works, see "An Individual Flips the Frame" and "A Team Flips the Frame" at the end of this chapter.

6.8: Plan Primary Learning First

Some teachers spend a lot of planning time on window dressing, making elaborate slideshow presentations, creating or buying graphic organizers online, adding graphics to handouts, or cutting out supplemental manipulatives. Attending to a lesson's visuals is important, and creating or buying unique materials is often fun for the teacher. On the other hand, if the teacher doesn't produce lessons with high-quality content and delivery, the students won't benefit.

Help the teacher focus their planning energy. Ask them if similar activities might already exist in the supplemental materials of the curriculum. Can students quickly draw a graphic organizer as part of the lesson instead of the teacher spending time photocopying one? Can teachers share lesson plans and materials? Is a slideshow presentation necessary in every class for students to comprehend the concept? Although graphics and animations are nice, that work should wait until the teacher has planned the primary learning tasks. Effective teachers are fierce editors of activities and materials superfluous to student learning.

6.9: Teach Coteachers to Plan

Some coteachers may plan successfully as individual teachers but not as a partnership. Lead them in a few rounds of planning. Suggest which coteaching model—for example, parallel teaching, station teaching, or one lead/one assist—they might use during which components of the lesson (DeRuvo, 2010). Introduce them to shared electronic documents to make the work more efficient.

6.10: Observe Planning

Watch a teacher's planning and look for common pitfalls. For example, do they focus more on activities or on precise student learning targets? Do they understand the concept they're attempting to teach? Do they consult their curriculum enrichment and supplemental materials? Have they carefully analyzed their students' data related to the lesson? Do they have common scaffolds readily available for English language learners or other students who might need them, such as writing frames, model answers, advance organizers, or word banks? Provide feedback to the teacher, especially if you note a pattern in the planning practice.

6.11: Script a Segment

If a teacher struggles with one aspect of the lesson—such as transitions, higher-level thinking questions, remediation, or formative assessments—have them write out precisely what they do and say and what the students do and say at those points in the lesson. Most teachers don't require a detailed plan for every task, but some benefit from carefully articulating trouble spots in instruction or the curriculum. Let them know they'll probably only need to do this meticulous planning about half a dozen times before they become proficient and move to a more generalized approach.

6.12: Use Triple-Column Lesson Design

Make the teacher's learning visible with a lesson plan graphic organizer. Lemov (2021) advocated two-column lesson plans for teachers to indicate student actions alongside teacher actions. We've found that adding a third column is helpful when the teacher is trying to incorporate a new technique.

In the example shown in Figure 6.1, the teacher is working on making student participation mandatory. The teacher understands the concept of including active participation but is struggling to get all students to respond. The reminders of what to do, and when to do it, help get this practice into place.

6.13: Control Introductions and Transitions

Suppose the teacher struggles to get through a lesson within the allotted time. When this occurs, focus on the lesson's front end and transitions, the most common places teachers lose time. Some teachers spend more time than needed explaining vocabulary and goals at the beginning of the lesson. Although that's important, that part of the class should be briefer than teacher modeling, concept development, or student practice. Generate ideas for editing the lesson opening using a timer or following strict time allocations. In addition, well-planned and practiced transitions, such as collecting papers and moving through labs, add valuable instructional minutes to each day.

Figure 6.1   Triple-Column Lesson Design

Teacher Actions	Student Actions	Targeted Skill or Strategy
Post the activator.	Students write responses in their notebooks.	Pace the class and take attendance, ensuring that all students write.
State the lesson objective and rationale.	Students chorally repeat the objective.	Scan the room, looking for everyone to speak. Repeat the process once or twice if needed.
Demonstrate the first problem.	Students copy the teacher model.	Tell students to write. Scan the room to see who is and isn't writing.
Practice 4–6 problems. Rotate between the teacher leading and students leading the problem steps. Stop and check everyone's steps along the way. Combine more problem steps in each new example.	Students complete problems step-by-step with the entire class. Students check one another's work. They discuss the errors they made and how to correct them in the following problem.	Pace the room to ensure that everyone completes all steps to all problems. Focus on what to do, not on what not to do. For example, instead of saying, "Archie, you're not working," say, "Archie, complete step 2 now" or "Archie, pick up your pencil."

6.14: Coplan and Coach

The approach of coplanning combined with coaching borrows heavily from the microteaching strategy. It involves rounds of abbreviated teaching episodes where the instructor demonstrates a technique with students and receives feedback from the coach (Allen & Eve, 1968; Leong et al., 2021). *Micro* refers to the amount of time (10–20 minutes), the number of students, and the fact that only one part or component of the lesson or curriculum is under consideration. In other words, the coach and teacher practice and analyze only a small aspect of teaching. This idea of coplanning and coaching extends easily into complete lessons or units. If the teacher requires additional supports, consider the strategy *engage in ICU: intensive coach use.*

6.15: Engage in ICU: Intensive Coach Use

Our experience reveals that some teachers underestimate the depth or amount of thinking that virtuoso teachers put into dynamic instruction. In-class instruction is analogous to watching a concert. What transpires in front of students is often the result of extensive preparation, rehearsal, and thought. For this reason, it's imperative for coaches to articulate and model the thought process and work involved in effective planning. ICU—intensive coach use—occurs in eight or more coaching rounds for eight weeks minimum, which translates to approximately three to six hours a week observing, planning, and coaching the teacher. Ideally, after a few rounds of coplanning, the coach steps back. In subsequent planning sessions, the teacher describes their thinking process as *they* lead the planning process. Coach observation and feedback follow each round of planning. Here are some tips on applying the ICU format:

- This is an intensive and time-consuming process for both the coach and the teacher. Consider other less strenuous coaching interventions before resorting to this practice. Also, consider the number of teachers you coach. You may not have enough time to coplan and complete ICU rounds with several teachers at once.

- Plan entire lessons or units of study as needed. Vary the breadth of the planning according to the teacher's and students' needs.
- If the teacher grapples with an entire lesson or unit, narrow your focus. For example, if a teacher can't demonstrate a strategy with the class or course as a whole, see if they can produce it with a small group of students. For example, in a primary classroom, if the teacher is struggling with checking for understanding, have them start with a small reading group and practice having students signal, show whiteboards, or use polling. With a secondary teacher, instead of asking the teacher to roll out a new curriculum with all their courses, start with their most manageable class. This is another example of *start small*.
- Provide feedback from recorded lessons.
- Conduct a think-aloud while you lead the planning with the teacher or, at a minimum, keep explaining the rationale behind your decisions as you plan. These are the most efficient ways to reveal the thinking behind lesson planning.
- While observing a lesson after coplanning, let the teacher know you might jump in to provide feedback out of earshot of students (Whisper Coach) or offer to coteach and quickly demonstrate a practice (Coteach Coach). Make sure you discuss these options ahead of time with the teacher; don't surprise them midlesson. The teacher may even let students know in advance that you'll interject during the lesson. You can find descriptions of both Whisper Coach and Coteach Coach in Chapter 8.

- Sometimes practices don't transfer from one setting to another. For example, an elementary teacher might plan and execute all the best moves for teaching reading but fail to use similar practices in mathematics. A high school teacher might gain proficiency in planning one course but continue ineffective planning in other classes. Don't be surprised when this occurs. The good news is that once the teacher shows they can produce the work, they probably can move the new learning to another setting. Simply shift the ICU process into the new arena. Often, the process moves more quickly in the new context.

- If the teacher doesn't demonstrate any improvement after intense coplanning and coaching in six to eight weeks, consider dropping this coaching intervention. As in medicine, the ICU is a short-term intervention, not a yearlong or multiyear process. Don't stop coaching the teacher; just place them back into the regular coaching cycle of about one or two coaching sessions a week.

The ICU work takes a great deal of time on the part of the coach. Remember, coaching isn't the remedy for every issue inside a classroom. Sometimes the problem needs other supervisory interventions. We've encountered several schools that poured all their coaching resources into a handful of the highest-need teachers while neglecting the rest of the staff, who needed assistance as well. Many coaches and administrators of high-needs teachers keep them in some form of intensive coaching for the entire school year in hopes of improving the teacher's practice; this isn't necessary.

We experimented with this ICU process for several years, documenting which variables determined teacher improvement with the intervention. Over time, patterns emerged. First, if the process worked at all, teacher change occurred between six and eight weeks. This knowledge proved invaluable for leaders who were relieved to know there was no need for continual comprehensive coaching for an entire school year. Second, we noted that about 70 percent of the teachers improved with this practice. They became proficient teachers afterward, even though some may have teetered on the verge of termination at the beginning of the process. At first, the success rate hovered around 50 percent, but as we helped coaches and administrators improve their skills at coaching data analysis and lesson planning, the numbers grew closer to 70 percent.

Another trend we noted concerned the difference between novice and veteran teachers. New teachers responded to the ICU process more quickly and more consistently. Frequently, they needed two rounds of ICU in two different content areas or courses; all the same, they cemented the new learning in their everyday practice. Several novice educators who moved through ICU became, within a year or two, teachers of some of the highest-performing students on the campus.

As for veteran teachers, they also showed improvement within the eight-week timeframe; that variable didn't change. Unfortunately, many experienced teachers in ICU didn't later rise to become powerful catalysts of high student outcomes; they became proficient teachers adept at producing typical student growth each year. They moved from teachers who struggled to create any productive effects with students to teachers who produced average results. We've yet to see a high-needs, highly experienced teacher move through ICU and then become a teacher who gains two or three years of academic or social growth in students in one school year.

What we did see on several occasions were conversations with leaders in which veteran teachers became emotional as a result of their ICU work. For the first time in their career, they were relieved to fully comprehend their standards, their students' needs, and basic instruction. One 11-year veteran 2nd grade teacher in Bakersfield, California, explained through tears,

I'm so grateful for them [the principal coaching the teacher]. All those years, I just didn't get it when we were in those large trainings. I thought I wasn't smart enough. I couldn't really understand what they kept asking us to do. When the principal helped me one-on-one, I got it. I just needed it explained to me alone, without all that pressure.

When in doubt about whether a teacher can improve through ICU, try it. You just might be empowering that teacher and a generation of future students for years to come.

Some administrators use ICU for a few months before determining whether to renew a low-performing teacher. If a supervisor is on the fence about continuing a teacher's contract because of inconsistent performance, the intensive coaching process may let them know if coaching improves the situation or not, thus helping them solidify their decision. Figure 6.2 illustrates the broad steps in the ICU process.

Figure 6.2   Intensive Coach Use: The ICU

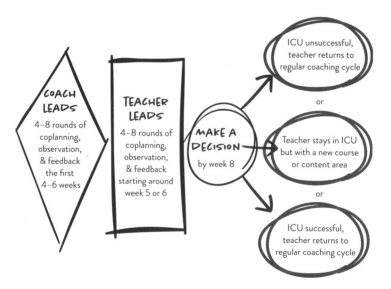

6.16: Ask Reflective Questions

Try any of the following reflective questions while planning with the teacher:

- What do you want students to show you at the check for understanding, the formative assessment? How will they do that? Let's start there and draft the objective and subsequent activities to match that picture.
- Which part of the lesson is an excellent place to give students leadership?
- What close confusers or misconceptions do you anticipate during the class?
- How might you modify this reading or activity for students who struggle during the lesson?
- If you were to rewind this lesson, what would you do differently?
- How can you get more students engaged in this part?
- How could we edit this part of the lesson so you have more time for other components?
- How are students going to get feedback during this part of the lesson?
- How might you get students to this point more efficiently or quickly?
- What do you want students to think about at this point in the lesson?
- What are some ways to make their thinking visible to you?

6.17: Use Others' Lesson Plans

For teachers new to the profession, new to teaching an age group, or new to a course, have them use lesson plans from teammates or another experienced teacher. This time-saving strategy can help new teachers get over a short-term hurdle or serve as a stopgap measure while they're learning appropriate planning strategies.

6.18: Edit the Lesson Plan

Encourage the teacher to use more straightforward activities and the shortest route to get students to learning targets. When we struggle with something, we often focus on aspects we can control, such as the font of a handout or the decoration of a learning station, or we'll dump a multiplicity of ideas into a simple guided-reading lesson. Doing something we can accomplish gives us a sense of control, but that type of extraneous work may be unnecessary for the lesson. Help the teacher know when to edit out ideas or issues—to take the shortest route—to focus on students' learning. To drive this point home, show them the simple graphic in Figure 6.3.

Figure 6.3   Edit the Lesson Plan: Take the Shortest Route

6.19: Manage Time

Time management and planning are essential partners. Teachers often use the term *overwhelmed*, which may refer to the fact that they haven't analyzed and organized their tasks to ensure they can accomplish them. Teach teachers that multitasking is a myth (Ophir et al., 2009; Parry & Le Roux, 2021); it actually lowers a person's IQ (Rock, 2020). Help them with general time management strategies.

The following are some tips to help teachers think about time usage:

- Identify the time you allot for specific activities using a *time audit*. Make sure to include socializing, gaming, watching TV, spending time on social media, playing with your children, meditating, or exercising—any activity vital to you.
- Identify "need to dos" as opposed to "want to dos."
- Talk about the process with your coach or a trusted colleague —someone who can be objective. Close friends and family tend to be very subjective and may provide you with all kinds of rationales to continue your current patterns.
- Find time for mindfulness rather than venting. As we pointed out earlier, venting may lead to depression (Yoon et al., 2017). Plan time to clear your mind rather than sitting and talking to others about how much you have to do.
- Experiment with time-saving strategies. Try the Pomodoro technique (or some other similar approach); this involves setting a timer for 20-minute intervals to focus your attention on completing a task. Experiment for a few weeks, 7–10 times, before deciding whether the tactic does or doesn't work for you.

6.20: Set a Timer or Two

Ask the teacher to experiment with using one or several timers during a lesson. One of those timers might be for the teacher to discover how much time they spend talking—giving directions, directing instruction, and so on—versus allowing students to talk and engage in tasks. Another timer might be set for an individual student to help keep them engaged in work. Even if the teacher is uncomfortable with this tactic, nudge them to experiment with it about a dozen times before they decide whether it's helping to increase student learning, student engagement, or their own efficiency.

6.21: Build on Teacher Strengths

Is the teacher a morning person? If so, have them conduct high-level thinking, such as planning and data analysis, in the morning. Do they work better on the weekends? Suggest they work on planning chunks over a weekend day. Author David Rock (2020) advocates matching your most productive time with the most complex tasks. His book, *Your Brain at Work,* uses the latest information from cognitive science for building work habits. Also, remove distractions, another strategy from Rock. Turn off the phone, mute text messaging, close social media alerts, and move to a place with minimal foot traffic. Rock makes it clear that multitasking doesn't work for most of us, particularly when we're conducting nonmenial tasks.

6.22: Delay Nonessential Tasks

Teach teachers how to politely and assertively manage requests on their time. Just because someone communicates a need, it isn't necessarily urgent. Check the calendar and have a place in your schedule for when you'll complete specific tasks. For example, a parent may ask for work for their child to take on vacation the following week; you don't have to perform that task at that moment. Instead, consider replying, "I can get those materials out to you on Thursday afternoons." Most of us do this naturally with our daily tasks. We don't do laundry every time a piece of clothing is dirty. We wait until enough clothing will fill the washer, plan for time to be home to move it to the dryer, and frequently dry the clothes in the evening when the temperature is cooler. Delaying tasks is different from procrastination; delaying uses time wisely and enables you to perform duties when it makes the most sense.

6.23: Research Planning with Outstanding Peers

Ask the teacher to survey four or five outstanding teachers about how they schedule their work and planning time. When the teacher reports back, help them craft a plan to implement the best ideas they unearthed. Frequently, teachers are surprised at the simple solutions their veteran colleagues have crafted over the years. Likewise, those experienced teachers are often teachers to the core; they enjoy teaching their efficiency tips to colleagues.

6.24: Review General Expectations

Provide the teacher with models of student work, learning progressions charts, developmentally appropriate practices, and typical expectations for the students with whom they work. Sometimes teachers overreach the standard or, conversely, maintain low expectations for students because they're unaccustomed to seeing typical work products or student outcomes.

6.25: Analyze Data

Help the teacher understand the assessments and results of the tests they use. Here are some common pitfalls for the teacher to avoid:

- **Lack of alignment.** Are the assessment questions aligned to the curriculum? Does the assessment align both the content and the thinking required? We often see that the level of thinking required of students on an assessment item doesn't match the level of thinking they encounter in the classroom around the same topic. When that happens, always reach for the higher level of thinking. For example, the assessment may ask students to analyze a character's growth over the course of the novel. By contrast, the classroom assignments might focus on what the character looks like and what happens along the plot line. This is a misalignment of the assessment and classroom instruction.

- **Shallow analysis.** Look deeply at who failed and *why*. Did all students select the same wrong answer, or were there outliers? Did some students blow off the assessment and now need one-on-one interventions instead of reteaching? Identify which part of the topic or concept students mastered and which aspect proved a struggle.
- **No reteach plan.** If the teacher has no plan to reteach topics after reviewing the data, reteaching is unlikely to occur (Bambrick-Santoyo, 2019).
- **An overly complex reteach plan.** We often find students need one of three or four things in reteaching. They need
  - » The concept modeled differently.
  - » More practice.
  - » Small-group work.
  - » Practice on a tiny part of a skill or concept, a step in a procedure, a misconception, a vocabulary review, and so forth. The reteach work is typically straightforward, not complex; students don't usually need the teacher to reteach an entire lesson to them or move them to an entirely new curriculum or piece of software. Analyze student errors carefully, and plan to reteach around that targeted scrutiny.
- **Taking data personally.** Some teachers take assessment results as a personal insult instead of as an indicator that a different student or teacher action needs to occur. To help the teacher overcome this, tell them to think about the fuel gauge on their car. When they see the fuel is near empty, they don't usually beat themselves up for not noticing earlier, nor do they ignore the fuel indicator by placing a smiley face sticker on it. They simply make a plan to get fuel. Similarly, coach the teacher to look at data results as an indication that a change

needs to occur. Don't ignore the data, don't beat yourselves up over the data, and don't blame others for the data. Just make a plan to address them.

6.26: Coplanning Lessons with a Group

Coplanning with a grade-level or content-area group has a greater effect in less time than coplanning individually with every teacher on a team. Also, it enables the coach to differentiate and use collective teacher expertise to improve practice. Decide on a simple agenda template that will work for the group. Start by preparing two or three planning formats, letting the team select their favorite. This move provides appropriate choice in team coaching; remember, wanting options is a characteristic of adult learners (Knowles et al., 2020). Model your expectations for planning. Suggest teachers plan alone, with a partner, or in small groups. (Again, you're sliding in options there, mindful of adult learner needs.) Covey (2020) recommends always starting planning with the end in mind. Encourage team conversation about what outcomes they expect from their students or how the students will show their learning in the formative assessment. Make that the focal point of each lesson.

6.27: Script DOK 3 Questions

With the exception of foundational skills, most lessons should aim for a minimum of DOK 2 thinking (Webb, 2002, 2007). Our experience revealed that most teachers are pretty proficient at planning activities, teacher questions, or student goals at that level, which includes basic reading comprehension skills, basic data interpretation, or multistep calculations in mathematics. Teachers struggle more with teacher queries and student work production at DOK 3. Prompts at this level don't just occur to teachers off the cuff; they take more careful thought. We suggest that teachers always plan one or two DOK 3 questions, even if the primary goal of the lesson is to produce thinking at DOK 2. When planning questions, the teacher needs to implement strategies that enable all students to respond, including dual-language learners and students with special needs.

Regularly planning DOK 3 questions is important for a couple of reasons. First, the students may be ready to produce DOK 3 thinking unbeknownst to the teacher. With DOK 3 questions planned in advance, the teacher is ready to move the students forward. Second, continually planning DOK 3 questions builds the teacher's capacity to articulate definitive DOK 3 inquiries, maybe even spontaneously. Instead of asking, "Who invented the telephone?" ask, "What problem did the creator of the telephone solve?" or "What problems did the inventor create?" Instead of asking for the answer to 20 × 15, ask, "How many ways can you determine 20 × 15?" or "What way is most efficient and why?" Instead of asking for the main idea of a paragraph, consider asking, "How might you use the paragraph in an argument?"

6.28: Consider All Aspects of Students as Learners

This strategy appeared in Chapter 2 as an equity tactic. It also works well as a general planning intervention. Ignoring the typical labels of "special education," "gifted," "language learner," and so on, request the teacher describe in writing how each of their students learns. Is the student addicted to reading? Do they watch everything you and their classmates do before they attempt work? Do they learn through gaming blogs? Do they use religious or spiritual analogies? Does the student grasp concepts quickly? Can the student practice with speed once they understand the concept? Do they make up slogans or acronyms to help them recall information? Do they want to jump in and practice before they read about something? Are they a leader? Do they learn from cosplay, rap, or board games? Do they relate most new things they learn to how their family functions? Do they make lots of connections to current events? Do they use two or three languages while learning? With these detailed notes in hand, jump into the planning and craft a lesson for the class based on the unique learning preferences of the students in the group.

What It Looks Like in Practice

An Individual Flips the Frame

Focus Strategies:
- Use triple-column lesson design
- Ask reflective questions
- Flip the frame of planning

When Angela was working with a high school teacher team, a new science teacher told her how they planned every lesson. The teacher showed Angela the textbook and explained how it recommended planning a lesson. This teacher followed the suggested plan closely, occasionally changing the time allotted for an activity because their students tended to be "low." Most of the other teachers agreed they did the same thing.

Angela asked them to take out their rosters and list their students by their initials. Next to each initial, they were to describe each student as a learner, not just in terms of their label (special needs, language learner, 504 plan). What made the student distinctive? Were they an internal or external processor? Did they prefer learning part to whole or whole to part? Was the student a good listener, or did they prefer to watch modeling? The teachers spent quite a bit of time working on the questions and adding their unique insights. When they finished, one person asked about the purpose of the activity. Angela replied, "Do you plan for content—or for them?" The consensus revealed they planned for content. The team spent another two hours preparing a lesson for the learners. Angela introduced *use triple-column lesson design* so they could track the way students engaged in the lesson and assess if it fit the students' needs. She also used *ask reflective questions* as they planned: How might you modify...? How will you engage...?

The next day, Angela observed some of the teachers. The new science teacher displayed sheer joy during the observation. The students were highly engaged, and they were definitely working hard. The teacher couldn't believe how planning *for* students changed their approach to the lesson. The simple method of *flip the frame of planning* empowered the teachers through planning.

A Team Flips the Frame

 Focus Strategies:
- Analyze data
- Flip the frame of planning

In Phoenix, Arizona, a 4th grade team needed help with their plan for reteaching inferencing in reading comprehension. All the students in the grade level had failed the formative assessment, and the teachers were confused as to why. Keith led the team in *analyze data*. They started by examining the formative assessment item and comparing it to the standard; there was alignment. Then the group reviewed individual student written responses. Almost all the students had attempted to respond; although they grasped the literal meaning of the text, they didn't grasp any implied meaning. Keith asked about the lessons leading up to the assessment. The group described the story that students had read for practice making inferences. This was the same story the teacher had used to introduce the concept. The students only practiced inferencing once, and the teachers had led that practice. They had not facilitated the independent practice of drawing inferences using any additional texts.

The teachers remarked, "But it was so hard just to get them to understand this one text!" When the group reviewed the text, they realized that although it was engaging, it was way too long; they needed multiple, shorter texts for students to use in practice. To gain independence in the skill, students needed to practice both with the teacher and independently. Teachers used the strategy *flip the frame of planning* for the reteach work by thinking about what each student needed to master the standard, starting with independent student work.

8th Grade Experts

Focus Strategies:
- Analyze data
- Ask reflective questions

A group of experienced, highly proficient teachers in San Diego, California, planned to show how their 8th grade team produced a common set of lessons, demonstrated high-quality instruction, and analyzed student work products. The group worked on these goals for a couple of weeks; they were to show a group of visiting coaches, principals, and lead teachers how they conducted professional development as a team. They were highly skilled at team planning and were demonstrating how to teach analysis of the author's use of point of view, with individual students writing paragraphs by the end of the lesson.

Keith and the visitors observed the lessons in several classrooms throughout the day. The 8th grade teacher hosts were going to model their analysis of student work at the end of the day. Because most students were learning English as a second language and many struggled to comprehend most of the texts written for the 8th grade level, the teachers provided multiple supports. Writing independently proved challenging for the entire grade level that year. Again, the teachers provided scaffolds for the individual writing work that students would produce at the end of the lesson. The array and skillfulness of the teachers' instructional strategies were stunning.

However, there was a problem. After a couple of observations, the observers noted that the final written product didn't explain how the students analyzed point of view; it simply summarized the passage. Although a written summary is a satisfactory outcome for 8th grade, it wasn't these teachers' intended and posted goal. The students' final written products didn't align with the lesson goal, the teacher model, and the student practice demonstrated in each lesson.

To move this experienced group of teachers forward, Keith decided to use two strategies from this chapter: *ask reflective questions* and *analyze data*. For the demonstration at the end of the day, Keith used reflective coaching. After offering several positive descriptions of what he had observed in the classrooms, he led a critique of student work. He asked, "What positive trends do we see in their writing? What needs to improve? Who demonstrated the goal of the lesson?" The group sorted the writing and dived into the analysis. In about 20 minutes, one of the teachers noted, "Oh no, our prompt was wrong." As a group, they figured out the writing prompt didn't solicit their desired outcome; it was misaligned with the lesson goal. They asked students, "What literary devices did Mark Twain use in *The Celebrated Jumping Frog of Calaveras County* to make you laugh?" The standard, however, stated, "Analyze how differences in the point of view of the characters and reader (created through the use of dramatic irony) create such effects as suspense and humor." They came to realize that they had worked so hard that year getting students *to write anything* that they simply neglected to check the alignment in this lesson. "Point of view" was completely absent from the prompt. They made a plan to correct the team error the following week. This story highlights the fact that even experienced, highly skilled teams may make errors aligning lesson activities with lesson goals and may need coaching assistance from time to time.

Coaches, Consider This...

- Which strategies from this chapter piqued your interest in coaching lesson planning with teachers? Why?
- How might you use the ICU strategy of intensive coaching around planning (or some adaptation of it) with a teacher you coach?
- What strategies from this chapter might help you coach teachers' thinking behind their lessons and lesson outcomes?
- How will you encourage teachers to use one of these strategies to plan for their students' needs rather than for the curricular needs?

7

Coaching Team Membership

Teaching exists in collaboration with groups of students, sets of parents, teams of teachers, and other social settings. Both Costa and colleagues (2016) and Kim and colleagues (2019) noted that a vital perspective for educators was working well in group environments. According to Costa, effective teachers are flexible enough to consider others' opinions about their work. Receptivity to teamwork and team input is crucial to how many professional learning communities (Little, 1993), grade-level teams, or departments operate in today's schools.

Often, the work of helping a teacher get along in groups falls to the coach. The ideas in this chapter provide coaches with the skills to help teachers function well in team settings.

Researcher	Effective Teacher Traits or Dispositions Related to Team Membership
Costa et al. (2016)	• Flexibility: sees other perspectives, adapts, changes • Interdependence: values relationships with others, desires community and reciprocity
Hattie (2012)	• Monitors learning and provides feedback

Researcher	Effective Teacher Traits or Dispositions Related to Team Membership
Kim et al. (2019)	• Extraversion: sociable, assertive, energetic • Emotionally stable: calm, secure, and tolerant of stress

Strategies

7.1: Start Small

Frequently, the social nature of teams makes wholesale change a staggering task. When helping a team function more effectively or with more heart, consider focusing on small changes first. Perhaps introduce the notion of including two or three meeting norms or a detailed advance agenda for meetings before tackling how to manage challenging behaviors or equitable discussion in teams. As with coaching individuals, a small positive result for a group often paves the way for receptivity to further team development.

7.2: Build Alliances

Some new teachers who work in high-needs schools report they feel among the minority in terms of beliefs about students and student learning. In other words, they see themselves as one of the few on staff who believes that all students can achieve the school's challenging academic and social goals. With a teacher such as this, suggest they wait before making allies among the staff. Often, if the teacher waits a few months, they'll hear comments in team meetings, and they'll listen to other colleagues talk about staff members. Once they have enough data, they can decide which teachers' ideals line up with theirs. Peers have a tremendous influence on teachers, so it's wise to carefully select who to formally or informally partner with.

7.3: Do Advance Work

Work with the teacher to identify the topic of upcoming team meetings, and have them prepare appropriately. Help the teacher prepare for the meeting to shore up their knowledge and ensure their participation. If the department or grade level plans to complete work on standards, then help the teacher dissect the standard beforehand; study common misconceptions around that standard; review the level of thinking required; and consider state, local, or national assessment items related to the standard. If the next team meeting involves analyzing student data, walk the teacher through an analysis of their student results first so they can put the analysis into context. If the upcoming grade-level team is reviewing student work samples, help the teacher select examples from their students—an exceptional model, a sample with common errors, an outlier example, and so on.

7.4: Prepare and Differentiate Professional Development

If the teacher is attending upcoming training, off or on site, help them make the most of the learning by reviewing the outcomes in advance. Provide readings or background knowledge to help accelerate performance once they're back in the classroom. Consider sending teachers to training in pairs or small groups. When they have someone to talk with, they may be more likely to consider specific methods to enact the practice.

One size does not fit all in professional development. Coaches need to consider what teachers need and how teachers learn. This doesn't mean that whole-group instruction isn't an option. However, professional development should be threaded with conversation, seek answers to real problems, and provide time for application. During those times, the coach should spend more time with novice teachers who may possess a smaller repertoire of tools. The coach may also prepare a group of novice teachers beforehand with some specific ideas to share. Give veteran, successful teachers leadership roles, and have them share or demonstrate their learning during small- or whole-group instruction.

We observed examples of differentiated professional development in several places. Some schools included professional development menus that gave teachers choices of topics labeled "pro" and "beginner." One school offered "expert groups"; teachers selected topics they were skilled in and shared their expertise with others who wished to become experts. One district arranged topics by course numbers—101, 201, 301, and so on—in ascending order by depth and complexity, which enabled everyone to self-assign by interest and experience.

7.5: Debrief Professional Development

Many teachers returning from intensive training are eager to implement new activities in their classrooms. Plan a debrief with the teachers following training. Help them review the activities they learned and vet how the new strategies match their students' current needs and the curriculum's demands. Be cautious of excitement over activities that don't fit student needs. Without curbing a teacher's enthusiasm, try to help them be wise consumers of training ideas and appropriately match activities with objectives and curriculum targets.

7.6: Clarify Meeting Purposes

Sometimes the general intention of a meeting is unclear. Similarly, an agenda item may reveal no solid objectives. To empower the teacher for full engagement, suggest they ask for clarity regarding the meeting agenda. For example, they might ask any of the following questions: "Are we making a decision about this right now, or are we making a recommendation that someone else will make a final decision about?" "Is the idea just to brainstorm right now and pick a solution later?" "Are we making a plan, or are we just venting? I just need to clarify." We noticed frustration when teachers thought their actions in a meeting were going to lead to a policy change or a solution and then found out that it wasn't the case. Helping the teacher clarify the purpose of meeting activities lets them know how intensely to focus and what the potential outcome of the meeting will be; it helps them function more productively as teammates. Figure 7.1 shows how one high school leadership team regularly includes a justification for each meeting agenda item.

7.7: Clarify Meeting Action Items

Teach the teacher to be clear about their responsibilities after any meeting. Tell them to double-check expectations. Keeping personal notes and simply asking about responsibilities before the end of the session help clarify who is expected to do what. An organizer for notes might help them keep track of the group's progress. Suggest that they offer to lead the group in the use of shared documents and that the group rotate the role of note taker at each meeting.

7.8: Set Up a Community of Practice

Some people work more effectively in small groups. They like to bounce ideas off others, not just you, the coach. They enjoy the camaraderie of colleagues and talking with those working in the same subject or with the same age group. A community of practice is a small study group of people who share a concern or a passion for something they do; they want to meet together regularly to learn how to improve their work (Wenger, 1999). Consider setting up a community of practice for your gregarious teachers who thrive when engaged with a small team.

Figure 7.1   Sample Meeting Agenda

Here is an agenda for a half-day high school department professional learning community session.

THE AGENDA TOPICS ARE IN BOLD

THE RATIONALE OR EXPLICIT PURPOSE OF EACH AGENDA ITEM FOLLOWS THE TOPIC, WHICH IS IN BOLD.

THIS TEAM HAS ONE PERSON WHO IS THE TIMEKEEPER; THE FACILITATOR ROLE ROTATES AMONG THE MEMBERS, AND ONE PERSON TAKES NOTES ON A SHARED DRIVE TO WHICH EVERYONE HAS ACCESS.

THIS GROUP ROTATES FACILITATORS FOR EACH SEGMENT OF THE MEETING.

ONE PERSON VOLUNTEERS TO LEAD THE OPENING AND CONNECTOR. THEN ANOTHER PERSON LEADS TEXT COMPLEXITY AND SO FORTH.

Session Agenda

Time	Topic	Facilitator
8:30	**Opening & Connector** to build camaraderie	
8:45	**Text Complexity** to review our definition of text complexity	
9:00	**Data Analysis** to conduct a broad analysis of student results on text-dependent questions from the last department formative assessment	
10:00	**BREAK**	
10:30	**Text-Dependent Questions** to practice writing TDQs for upcoming lessons	
11:15	**Closing & Sharing of TDQs**	

7.9: Carry the Calendar

Coach the teacher to get into the habit of taking their calendar—electronic or paper—with them to every single work meeting. Tell them to schedule all activities regardless of how small. Help the teacher become proficient with the district's electronic platform and the integration of notes, to-do lists, calendars, and shared documents. These simple actions of toting the calendar around and learning a few electronic tools help preclude overcommitting and unnecessary follow-up about schedules.

7.10: Take Notes

Encourage teachers to take notes during meetings and professional development to increase their learning (Peper & Mayer, 1986) and to help them stay focused on the topic. Encourage note taking during coaching sessions as well. Also, make sure the teacher is familiar with the research that says that handwritten notes are more effective for retaining information than electronic notes (Mueller & Oppenheimer, 2014; Umejima et al., 2021). Several apps and programs are available to convert handwritten notes to electronic files, if the teacher prefers compiling them in this way.

7.11: Balance Participation

Coach the teacher on how to balance their involvement in a group. For new teachers, this may be the first time they've participated in work team meetings, so learning this vital skill may not be intuitive. They need to speak up when necessary and not take too much airtime during group discussions. If required, observe them in a meeting and provide feedback afterward. For more resources on how to balance individual participation in group meetings, see Aguilar (2016), Shapiro (2015), or Smutny (2019).

7.12: Reduce Venting

If unmitigated griping is a norm in the school or occurs with a specific teacher, brainstorm some strategies for politely exiting conversations or changing the discussion's direction. Helping teachers with their assertiveness skills improves their work group performance and enhances their general social skills and mental health.

Continued complaining is like trying to plant a tree in solid bedrock with a rubber mallet. You can continue to hit the rock until your arm is sore and your back hurts, but you won't have come any closer to planting the tree. To get the job done and enjoy the coolness of the shade, find out how to remove the rock, get the right tools, and plan to make the necessary changes.

7.13: Deal with Challenging Teammates

In most cases, everyone is a challenging person to someone else. That said, teachers often need help dealing with difficult teammates. The following are a few typical situations and solutions:

- **The dominator.** Try looking away from the person dominating the conversation and directly at someone else, and ask, "Let's hear your ideas on the topic" or "I'd love to hear others' views." Also, ask the leader to provide time limits and group norms about *equitable voice* for the meetings.

- **The bully.** Ignore them. If a teacher makes comments such as these—"You're too young to know; get some more experience, and you'll know better." "That'll never work; we tried that before." "Whose side are you on, the administration's?"—try *fogging* (Rigby, 2012). Don't defend yourself; instead, offer vague responses like, "Hmm, you might be right," "Could be true," or "Perhaps." When the person doesn't get their typical desired response—a return argument or anger from you—they often stop the behavior. It may take a few attempts before they stop. If you want, follow fogging with a push to continue the conversation: "You're right; I probably don't have the experience needed; let's discuss this idea anyway, and see if others want to try it." Another tip to remember for bullies comes from Stone and Heen (2014). Confront the behavior, not the personality. Don't remark, "You're a jerk." Instead, say, "You did/said _____. That behavior has to stop." Be prepared to stand your ground because the bully often makes excuses. They might suggest the real problem was "the situation," "your oversensitivity," or "the timing." Just respond, "Regardless of _____ (the situation, timing, and so on), that behavior has to stop."

- **The person who goes off topic.** Try moving their idea to a different time. Comment, "That's an interesting notion; can we move that to the end of the meeting?" or "Can we address that at our next session?"

- **The person who is oppositional.** Try getting more details. If someone opposes your professional viewpoint, try probing. Respond, "Tell me more about this; it's very different from my experience" or "If you could explain what you mean in detail, then I might be able to get on board with your thinking." This approach may help you uncover their motivations or logic—or even flawed assumptions. Either way, it may help keep the conversation going instead of just producing a stand-off and stopping the discussion.

- **The slacker.** For the person who doesn't pick up their part of the group task, try the following. Make sure the meeting minutes include explicit agreements with firm timelines and outcomes. Be prepared to accept less-than-stellar work; don't jump in and do the work for them even if it's not up to your quality standard. Also, have someone on the team assume the role of check-in provider, a person who reminds others of approaching deadlines, either in person or by email. Finally, regularly review team goals to make sure that everyone can actually complete the tasks.

- **The person who makes assumptions or goes to the extremes.** This person might state something like "What do you mean? You want us to give up our Saturdays and come in here to sell donuts?!" Clarify your intent (Stone & Heen, 2014): "I didn't intend to say _____. I *did* intend to say _____."

- **The person who raises their voice or sounds angry.** Try the word *passion.* "I appreciate your passion for this topic. I feel strongly about it as well." If needed, let them know you'd like them to lower their voice. Sometimes, just labeling their anger as passion is enough to help them calm down so the team can continue to function.
- **The interrupter.** Try patience, but also finish your thought or let someone else finish theirs. Consider responding, "I'm glad our ideas are flowing, and I want to hear what you have to say, but I'd like to finish my thought" or "Can you hold on to your idea? Before we move on, I would really like to hear where Shelley's thought was going."

Some leaders jot down these strategies with the intention of using them during a meeting; this way, they don't have to rely on their memory.

Don't worry if you don't like confronting people; most people typically don't like confrontation either. Many teacher leaders tell us they're not so intimidated by their colleagues after trying a couple of these approaches. Many of these scripts get people to work more productively as a team. Also, remember that most people aren't thinking about us as much as we believe they are; it's called the *spotlight effect* when we overestimate how much others are focused on us (Gilovich & Savitsky, 1999). So experiment with strategies for confronting those confounding teammate behaviors. Then try not to obsess too much over those issues. For an example of how a team managed a challenging team member, see "A Team Manages a Colleague—And the Team as a Whole" at the end of this chapter.

7.14: Value Other Philosophies

Many adults are not going to agree on differences in basic philosophies or beliefs. Teach the teacher to recognize differences among the educational philosophies they maintain and those of their team-mates. Healthy discussion of differing theories may prove stimulating and may be necessary for some work. Other times, it's best not to argue those issues too much. Just acknowledge the difference and move on, especially if the issue bogs the team down and taking a position on the different philosophies isn't relevant to completing the group work. Try, "That's a different belief, not one that I hold, and that's fine." In art shows, a group of artists will look at the same still-life model and paint it simultaneously with different results. All the paintings are art, and all communicate, just with different styles.

7.15: Watch a Team

If you need a grade level to implement a strategy that one or two teachers from another grade level are implementing well, coach them in a group setting. In the Learning Forward video *Ford Middle School: PD in Action* (www.youtube.com/watch?reload=9&v=T8F04i D4Yc8), a group of math teachers demonstrates this with great skill. This multigrade team of teachers uses data to investigate their own teaching practices. When they discover that one of the teachers on the team is being more successful than others with a particular standard, they agree to observe the teacher and discuss what occurred, resulting in a change of teaching strategy for all.

7.16: Manage the Change Process

Another source of challenging adult behaviors stems from the change process. Researchers Hall and Hord (2019) provided a practical approach to managing change. For example, at the beginning of a change, groups might inquire, "What is this exactly?" or "Aren't we already doing this?" Then they start thinking about how the change directly affects them and how they might manage the new issue. Finally, the group moves through a more transformational process when they start thinking about the consequences of the change, collaborating with others, and refining the change.

The change process affects teachers in various ways. If a team of teachers is requested to collaborate on a new topic with no time to address initial implementation questions or adapt the new idea into their work, there's bound to be conflict. Coach the teacher leader to listen carefully to what others are asking about a recent change. To encourage teachers to feel free to talk, give an example of a time you had concerns about a change, what your concerns were, and why. If concerns are primarily about implementing this new idea into the existing curriculum, address that concern fully before forcing the group to focus on other topics, such as how the issue affects student outcomes.

Hall and Hord (2019) look at seven stages of concern about change. Figure 7.2 shows a summary of that process. Typically, people gradually move from the lowest level to the highest one, but everyone moves at different paces, and sometimes people get stuck at one point or another. The wise leader recognizes the stages and resolves issues around each concern before nudging the team or individual further along in the process. The implementation story "They Hate Me and Won't Stop Complaining!" at the end of this chapter illustrates how a teacher guided their team through change.

7.17: Consider Adult Learner Characteristics

Knowles and colleagues (2020) identified a bevy of characteristics that set adult learners apart from student learners. It's imperative to keep four or five of these traits in mind when working with teams of adults:

- **Adults tend to be self-directed learners.** They like to set the *when* and *how* when it comes to learning something new. Although it's not always feasible to give adults free rein or choice in their learning, you should add as many choices as possible. For example, offer in-class or out-of-classroom feedback for coaching work, ask if they prefer a direct or more facilitative discussion, or provide options for small-group or individual professional development activities. For teamwork, build in these options when possible. Let teachers brainstorm how they'll implement plans, suggest they rotate team member roles, allow a choice of deadlines, provide broad team targets, and enable them to decide how they'll reach the goal.

- **Adults possess a great deal of experience, and they value that experience.** Bring their ideas to the table for brainstorming or consulting on team issues. Encourage them to listen to experts or read the research and talk about how an approach does or doesn't align with their experiences.

Figure 7.2   Modified Concerns-Based Adoption Model (CBAM): Stages of Change

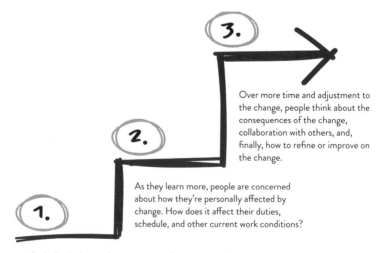

3. Over more time and adjustment to the change, people think about the consequences of the change, collaboration with others, and, finally, how to refine or improve on the change.

2. As they learn more, people are concerned about how they're personally affected by change. How does it affect their duties, schedule, and other current work conditions?

1. In the beginning, at the awareness and information levels, people are concerned about basic information: what is this change?

- **Adults tend to be goal oriented.** Set short- and long-term actionable tasks as a team.
- **Adults like to solve problems.** Make sure the teamwork focuses on addressing real issues the group is facing.
- **Adults prefer practical information.** Be sure that team actions help the group's students and the school's circumstances or program. Also, instead of just talking during team meetings, complete a task. A sense of completion makes a team meeting feel valuable.

Teach teacher leaders these specific characteristics. If you coach a struggling team, use these characteristics as a checklist to see if the team's work addresses these issues.

7.18: Assume Positive Intent

For productive communication in teams, teach the teacher about the powerhouse strategy of *assume positive intent*. Assuming positive intent means consciously selecting to believe our teammates are operating to the best of their ability and acting in the best interest of the school, team, or students (Bailey, 2011, 2015; Costa et al., 2016; Patterson et al., 2012).

Here's how the concept works. First, there's the account of what happened: a person slumps in their chair, makes no eye contact, and participates minimally. Those are just the *facts* of the story. Beyond the facts is the *theme* behind the story, what we assume, given those facts: the person doesn't want to be here; they're unhappy; they don't like this topic; they hate me; they're tired; they're in pain from recent surgery. We can decide to make the theme behind the incident negative or positive. Assuming there's a constructive or positive rationale behind any behavior helps get us to a calmer state for dealing with the behavior. When we assume that the other person's concerns are valid and when we operate from a space of compassion for them, we see things that weren't apparent earlier, and we often can be far more creative about how to move forward. For many people, this tactic takes practice to become second nature because our first inclination is often to assume hostile intent. Use and teach positive intent when coaching teams so they can improve group communication.

7.19: Don't Rush a Response

Teach the team they can always go back and restart a conversation. Sometimes, a teacher will encounter a challenging situation with a team member in a meeting and be uncertain how to respond. Later, on the drive home or the next day during morning coffee, they'll think of the perfect response. Encourage them to return to the challenging teammate and say, "I thought about what you mentioned in Thursday's meeting. Here's what I wish I had replied." Taking some time, even a few days perhaps, to confront a colleague might be a better tactic because nerves may be calmer and thoughts clearer. Even practicing what you want to express may help you become more explicit. (Yep, we're urging you to role-play again; do you notice a pattern?)

7.20: Mend Collegial Relationships

Sometimes when adults have strong disagreements, they tend to avoid each other for a while (sometimes years!). Encourage the team to work to repair their relationships as needed. For example, they could seek out the person they had differences with and try something like this: "Hey, Danuzia, I know we had a passionate disagreement at the team meeting yesterday. I just wanted to check in and make sure the two of us are OK." This might start a conversation that helps quell differences and mend bridges.

On the other hand, the answer to "Are we OK?" is frequently "no." If the relationship in question is between the coach and the teacher, the coach needs to step back and focus on that, saying something to the effect of "I'm sorry to hear that. What might help us get back on track?" or "I respect your feelings; I hope we can problem solve together to make repairs. What's the first step I can take?" If there's still a roadblock, the coach may need to move to another route: "It sounds as though our working together right now is not going to be beneficial for you. Can you tell me the attributes you would like in a coach? Perhaps I can find someone who would be a better fit." The coach should *not* permit the teacher to opt out of being coached.

7.21: Hear When Adults Are Asking for Help

Some adults don't like to admit they don't know something. We've noticed this a great deal when coaching teams and, in particular, when coaching administrators. To communicate a need for a solution, they will often describe a situation or quote someone else. For example, instead of asking directly, "Give us some ideas for how to solve this problem," they'll explain a situation, such as "We have some teachers who do such-and-such," or they'll remark, "Our social studies department chair says _____." Then they stop talking.

This type of remark cues you to find out if they need solutions to the scenario. Query, "Do you want help with that?" "Should we problem solve that issue together?" "Do you want me to list some responses you might give when they say _____?" That last question proves pivotal because many times the person or team is hungry for words or scripts they might use; they can't think of an appropriate response for the circumstance, and they're hoping you have potential language for them. Listen carefully when a team or an administrator describes a scenario; it's often a request for assistance.

7.22: Adhere to Meeting Components

When advising teacher leaders or teams, make sure they know the essential components for productive team meetings. Many people skip these components if their team works well together, but these measures add efficiency, and if the group ever starts to have challenges as a unit, the team will appreciate these foundations.

Designate roles (Aguilar, 2016; Bambrick-Santoyo, 2019; Costa et al., 2016; Shapiro, 2015; Smutny, 2019; Van Velsor et al., 2010). Have a facilitator, note taker, timekeeper, and process observer. The facilitator keeps the work moving forward. The note taker posts the notes on the meeting electronically so anyone who needs them can access them afterward. The timekeeper reminds the group of the time allotments. The process observer lets the group know how the team did with the behavioral expectations during the meeting. These positions can rotate or stay in place for the school year or semester.

Decide on basic group norms (Aguilar, 2016; Bambrick-Santoyo, 2019; Costa et al., 2016; Shapiro, 2015; Smutny, 2019; Van Velsor et al., 2010) such as these: "We support all final decisions; we assume positive intent with one another; everyone shares, not just the loudest and most persuasive member." Ensure the norms address group needs; change them as the group develops, and ask the process observer to verbally report on the norms in each meeting.

Figure 7.3 shows one middle school's team meeting norms posted on a presentation slide. At each meeting, team members select one norm to target. They jot down the norm on a note and keep it nearby. Periodically, the group pauses and either in pairs or as a whole group, members report on how they're progressing on the selected norm. It only takes a couple of minutes to do this, and the activity helps the team develop their communication skills.

Have a simple agenda. Provide it ahead of each meeting, and use it as an outline for note taking (Aguilar, 2016; Bambrick-Santoyo, 2019; Costa et al., 2016; Shapiro, 2015; Smutny, 2019; Van Velsor et al., 2010). Identify any work that needs to be completed beforehand, such as grading student writing so the team can analyze it during the team meeting. Also, think of the agenda like a curriculum outline, with tiny objectives or rationales beside each item.

Figure 7.3   Sample Meeting Expectations

Be Present	**Respect the Conversation**	**Today's Norms Activity**
• On time • Prepared • No sidebars • No device interruptions	• Share the floor. • Engage in active listening. • Have positive intent. • Gently remind norms breakers.	At your table, nominate a norms tracker for the morning, and pick a norm to focus on. Write the norm on the back of your table tent as a reminder. We'll debrief norms throughout the morning.
Participate Actively • Clarify questions. • Disagree and push. • Give honest feedback. • Work toward resolution.		

For example, an item on the agenda might be to analyze the latest formative assessment. The explanation attached to the item might explain the purpose of the activity in this way:

- Broad Data Analysis (agenda item): initial analysis will look at standards met and unmet (agenda item rationale)

- Reteach (agenda item): examine patterns in student errors on recent assessment to develop small-group reteach strategies (agenda item rationale)

Include these rationales along with the agenda item; this helps people stay focused on the task at hand. In addition, empower teams with the strategies *manage the change process, consider adult learner characteristics,* and *deal with challenging teammates,* which we discussed earlier. These basics help groups work more competently.

7.23: Ask Reflective Questions

Ask any of the following reflective questions while coaching teachers to be part of a successful team setting:

- What are the characteristics of a successful team meeting? What is *your* role in that success?
- What are the common barriers to achieving a positive team atmosphere? Which two barriers are crucial to remove?
- When is the best time to build relationships with veteran teachers? With novice teachers?
- How do you communicate your needs or ideas in a team setting? Around what issues do you need to be more assertive? With what topics might you need to better align with the team's thinking?
- What personal behaviors in teams are most annoying to you? What tactics can you use to mitigate your irritation?
- How might you introduce to your teammates the notion of group norms or providing a detailed agenda?
- Who is not contributing or being ignored in your meetings? How can you get their voice into the conversations in an equitable manner?

- The school has decided to adopt a new curriculum. What's the first step you would like the school to address for you and other teachers on your team regarding this change?
- If you started a community of practice, what would be the topic? Who would you invite?
- What one or two approaches would make your team meetings more participatory, efficient, or brief?
- How do you show up prepared for a team meeting? What do colleagues need to do to prepare?

What It Looks Like in Practice

A Team Manages a Colleague— And the Team as a Whole

 Focus Strategies:

- Simply say it
- Don't rush a response
- Adhere to meeting components

Tamarra coached an elementary instructional leadership team in Southern California that devised a unique way of incorporating the special needs of a teammate. The team had worked together for a couple years and had issues with one team member—the 2nd grade chair—who was unable to stop talking and needed to convince the group that their own perspective was the correct one. The group had difficulty completing work; all the members complained about this teacher to Tamarra, their school coach. Tamarra asked the team leader if they had addressed the issue with the teacher. They had not; no one had tried the strategy *simply say it,* which Tamarra was recommending. After some rehearsal (*don't rush a response*), the leader met with the teacher alone to talk about the issue. It turned out that the teacher was happy to address it with the entire team.

The team met, and everyone discussed what they saw as the problem with a great deal of positive intent. Everyone appreciated much of what the 2nd grade teacher said in meetings. They valued the teacher's experience, but they couldn't tolerate the teacher's relentless need to defend a position that the majority didn't hold. The team members asked what they could do as a group to address this.

The teacher listened, took notes, and told the group that no one had ever told them this before and that they were grateful for the feedback. The teacher also said it would be helpful if someone could nudge them or touch their arm when this happened to alert them to stop. Everyone agreed, with another teacher adding, "This should be a norm for the entire group, not just the 2nd grade teacher. We all get a little too obsessive or emotional at times about our ideas." So the team created a norm for excessive emotional attachment to an idea. When this behavior surfaced, one team member would gently remind another with a touch or a word that "the point was made" and that it was time to talk less. To this day, if you observe this high-functioning team meet, you'll occasionally see someone touch another's forearm or whisper a prompt, "OK, enough." Is that a group expectation Tamarra would have suggested? No. But it's an excellent example of how a team can create a unique norm.

"They Hate Me and Won't Stop Complaining!"

 Focus Strategies:
- Manage the change process
- Deal with challenging teammates

Keith worked for several years in a high school in California. At one point, the beloved, long-time chair of the English department retired. The teachers voted for a new chair, another long-time department teacher, a veteran staff member with a patrician facade and a host of advanced degrees from prestigious universities.

Coincidentally, that same year the school adopted the new Common Core State Standards. The first time Keith met one-on-one with the new department chair in October, the chair immediately started crying.

The new chair said, "I don't know what's wrong with these people! They hate me and won't stop complaining. I've never seen anything like this. Most of these teachers are long-time friends of mine. I can't take this any longer; I'm going to resign as department chair." Keith acknowledged the chair's concern but then asked, "What exactly are they complaining about?"

He learned that all the teachers' complaints were about the Common Core: "What sets of novels can we use now?" "Where are all the resources for these new standards?" "How are we going to manage the formative assessment system?" The list went on and on. Keith and the chair started writing down the specific questions and complaints from the teachers. After several pages, Keith asked the chair to look at the list, wondering if they noted a pattern.

The new chair did, commenting, "These things are all very... *logistical!*" Bingo! With no exception, all the complaints were about getting resources or managing the new standards. Not one person complained about the validity of implementing the standards or the new department chair's personality, communication style, or leadership.

Keith whipped out the stages of change from Hall and Hord (2019), which we discussed in *manage the change process*. The two examined the change phases and noticed the department was at the earliest steps; the teachers were concerned with management and the effect of the new standards on them.

"If that's true, why am I feeling so attacked?" the chair asked.

Keith explained, "Your team members are extraordinarily sarcastic and use wicked wit. Try to find ways to ignore their biting remarks and rolled eyes; you can solve these issues." Calmer and empowered with a different perspective, the new chair agreed to give it a try.

Six weeks later, Keith returned and revisited the English chair. A changed person, the leader explained that they did exactly what they had discussed with the coach. They ignored their colleagues' rude attitudes flying around like dangerous campfire embers and focused on solving practical issues. The chair used *deal with challenging teammates*, along with some intentional ignoring and fogging. Much to Keith's surprise and in a very short time, the chair and the team gained entirely new dispositions and productively shifted to the new standards. The chair kept the leadership position and has led the department successfully since that time. Knowing the change process and how it might affect group work is a valuable tool for those coaching teacher leaders.

Coaches, Consider This...

- Think about the teams in your school or program. Which ones are the most and least effective? Do any teams need to experiment with the strategies suggested in this chapter?
- *Adhere to meeting components* lists a powerful set of ideas. How might any one of those ideas become a part of your skill set when you lead groups?
- Regarding a team you work with, how might you ensure everyone gets an "equitable voice" in the work? How would you solicit input from those who speak less frequently?

8

Tools That Will Help

This last chapter offers tools we've used in coaching work with thousands of coaches in multiple settings, both in the United States and abroad. The tools complement several of the strategies we've discussed in this book. Let's first look at Young's Coaching Apps, an invaluable format that will help coaches know what to say and when, adding order to their observations.

Young's Coaching Apps

Although many administrators and coaches we worked with attended lots of training in coaching, we found that few of them could deliver a focused coaching conversation or were comfortable having us watch them coach someone else. First, we found that people needed order to the conversations; they needed to know what to do at the beginning, middle, and end. Second, they needed to know how to shift from a positive or praise message to a more critical or reflective message.

Enter Young's Coaching Apps (see Figure 8.1), where we provide dialogue frames to guide the coach through each stage of the observed conversation. (Think of these as *applications*—that is,

Figure 8.1 Young's Coaching Apps: Four Dialogue Frames

App	Begin Conversation	Mid-Conversation	End Conversation
PDA App (Positive Descriptive Appreciation) Start with PDA. Then select one of the three apps below.	**State positive student outcomes.** *"The model the students received detailed the thinking required in the lesson."*	**Ask questions about the outcomes.** *"How did you get them to be so articulate?"* **Connect to best practice, the research base, or the schoolwide focus.**	**Encourage continuation.** *"Kudos! Your students need this every single day, every period!"*
1. Mini-Reflect App Go here for minor issues and briefer conversations.	**State students' missed opportunity.** *"There was an opportunity here for students to demonstrate DOK 2 thinking."*	**Discuss ideas to solve the student problem.** *"Brainstorm how to get them all writing."* **Get commitment to one solution.**	**Set a time to see implementation.** *"When will students be able to do this?"* **Get a summary:** *"Please recap our conversation."*

2. Major-Reflect App Go here for highly reflective teachers who possess numerous strategies.	**Ask general questions about student outcomes.** *"How did student thinking go?"*	**Ask specific questions to analyze the data.** *"What did you see from students to support that?"*	**Ask questions for a plan of action.** *"What concrete steps might solicit responses from all of the students?"* **Get a summary**: *"Please recap our conversation."*
3. Instruct App Go here for a significant missed opportunity.	**State students' major missed opportunity and its significance.** *"Students need instruction on grade level to meet the standards."*	**Teach the practice needed.** *"We'll role-play this strategy."*	**Set a time to see implementation.** *"When will students be able to do this?"* **Get a summary**. *"What are your big takeaways?"*

approaches to apply—as opposed to something you download on your mobile phone.) We've used this framework thousands of times with great success. Providing specific approaches with the four apps has helped coaches and administrators better track modeled conversations, and it has enabled us to provide more explicit feedback to them when they coach in front of us. Once we started working with more structure and the four apps, the coaches' and principals' skills in coaching soared, moving teacher and team practices forward.

Why call these four approaches *apps*? Each app takes into consideration the research on powerful feedback. Research on the change process (Hall & Hord, 2019) and adult learning theory (Knowles et al., 2020) undergirds each approach, as well as the steps in each conversation. In addition, the entire framework is grounded in situational leadership theory (Hersey & Blanchard, 1969; Northouse, 2022). As you can see, a complete conceptual framework supports these dialogue frames; the whole format is an operating system, if you will, that performs like the operating system of a phone. You don't always notice the functionality that the operating system brings to the phone, but there's no need to always know it; you simply use the apps that rely on the system.

The four coaching apps work similarly; beneath the structured exchanges and the specific dialogue steps sits rock-solid research. We refer to the apps as Young's Coaching Apps because Keith produced this most recent outline of our coaching dialogues.

The 18 Coaching Formats

The coaching apps structure the actual coaching dialogue, whereas the *coaching formats* determine when, where, and with what intensity we deploy the coaching conversations. We're big fans of differentiating coaching conversations and switching up when and where we coach teachers. Initially trained to preconference, clinically observe, script, and then sit one-on-one to coach teachers, we started experimenting with other coaching formats while at WestEd and while coaching preschool through 12th grade teachers in California. Shortly after that, we came across *Differentiated Literacy Coaching* (Moran, 2007) and *Teach Like a Champion 3.0* (Lemov, 2021), both of which outlined some of the coaching structures we adapted and found successful.

Following are the 18 coaching formats we use for coaching:

1. Sit Down, 1-on-1 Coach
2. Whisper Coach
3. Signal Coach
4. Coteach Coach
5. Asynchronous Coach
6. Micro Coach
7. Intensive Coach Use (ICU)
8. Model Peer Coach
9. Model Teach Coach
10. On-the-Fly Coach
11. Corridor Coach
12. Student Work Coach
13. Target Coach
14. Self-Coach
15. Team Coach
16. Peer Coach
17. Video Coach
18. Ramble Coach

When determining which coaching format to use, we consider three questions: (1) What do I need to consider about the setting or environment? (2) How much time do I have? and (3) Is the teacher a struggling, novice, or expert teacher?

Consider the Environment

If you're conducting Sit Down, 1-on-1 Coach with the teacher, you need a location to include a pre- or post-conference discussion. This structure also works well if you need to work with the teacher on instructional or data analysis planning issues. This format is the traditional model that comes to mind when most people think of coaching; the coach conducts classroom observations and analyzes student outcomes with the teacher.

Another coaching setting to consider is coaching live during instruction. The coach acts as a coteacher in class with Coteach Coach, providing explanations, displaying notes, taking student questions, and directing student engagement. The coach models a small segment of the lesson, a coaching point the teacher needs to see demonstrated. This structure requires coplanning with the teacher in advance and a debrief afterward so the coach can verbalize their thinking processes to the teacher.

Model Teach Coach is similar to Coteach Coach, but here, the coach models a practice or a complete lesson for the teacher. Require the teacher to coplan with you beforehand so they see the thought process behind the live model. Give the teacher a note-taking guide or a set of practices to observe during the model, and debrief after the model. If the teacher is willing, consider providing brief feedback during a break in instruction out of earshot of students. Do this with Whisper Coach or Signal Coach. In both cases, let the teacher know in advance this will happen. Conduct brief feedback verbally in person, using an earpiece, by text, or with a handwritten note (Whisper Coach), or signal the teacher with a whiteboard or using a gesture you've previously agreed on to cue a teacher action (Signal Coach). Live prompting is all the quick coaching some teachers need to move a practice into place.

The most intensive coaching format, Intensive Coach Use (ICU), involves a minimum of eight rounds of intensive coplanning, observing, and debriefing with the teacher over eight weeks. This format includes pre- and post-conferencing and may consist of brief coaching live during instruction, with the coach modeling in the classroom.

Micro Coach is similar to ICU, but it doesn't require such intensive coplanning from the coach; this structure is adapted from microteaching (Allen & Eve, 1968; Leong et al., 2021) and microlearning (Leong et al., 2021). The coach coaches a tiny slice of instruction, such as the student questioning techniques or how to give formative feedback, for 10–12 minutes. Use live or recorded instruction for observation and feedback with the teacher. Consider using Micro Coach with individuals or groups of teachers.

Another issue to consider is the availability of other teachers. Several coaching formats call on the use of peers or models for the coached teacher to observe. With Model Peer Coach, the coach goes with the teacher to observe another teacher model; the teacher doesn't go alone. The coach can provide verbal narration or an annotated note-taking guide during the observation. This focuses the teacher precisely on the practice they need.

Similar to Model Peer Coach, the format of Peer Coach requires less presence of the coach. The coach determines a structure for peers across teams to observe one another and provide feedback on student experiences and outcomes. Teachers may be from the same department or grade level or be in similar affinity groups, such as new teachers, department chairs, instructional leadership teams, special educators, or specialists. This format is powerful for working on curriculum fidelity practices, equitable instruction, or other common group goals. This model is *not* ideal for struggling and some novice teachers because they may need more precise coaching from traditional coaches or expert teachers.

Consider Time and Intensity

Another factor to consider when selecting a coaching format is the time and intensity you provide for coaching. Some coaches maintain large caseloads; they need to be reasonable about their time and make hard decisions about who to serve and how frequently. Some coaches are in schools with many high-needs teachers, where the demands of the coach are more extensive than in other schools. There's simply a finite amount of time in a school day and school year.

A couple of coaching formats require less time from the coach. Highly effective, expert teachers might coach themselves (Self-Coach). In this case, the coach provides a rubric, checklist, or set of questions that guide the teacher's self-reflection. The teacher might watch videos of their teaching or reflect on their students' work and set growth goals based on their analysis. Another approach to apply is On-the-Fly Coach. Here, the coach provides brief coaching interactions when only a minute or two is available for feedback, offering a solid appreciation message and one minor point for reflection or correction.

Two coaching formats allow the coach a bit more flexibility with their physical presence. Asynchronous Coach and Video Coach enable the coach to do some coaching work when teachers are not even in the building. With Asynchronous Coach, the coach leads lesson or unit plan reviews, a problem of practice, or a book study—virtually. The coach offers comments or questions, and the teacher interacts with that material by email or in a shared document. This process provides flexible timing for both teacher and coach and works well with highly skilled and very reflective teachers. With Video Coach, the teacher records a lesson; the coach previews the video and provides guiding notes about specific moments in the lesson that the teacher needs to review *before* they meet to coach. They then meet live or virtually to debrief the video data and set goals. Many coaches with teachers in remote or off-site locations find Asynchronous Coach and Video Coach invaluable alternatives to in-person coaching.

See Figure 8.2 for a continuum indicating the time and intensity involved with the 18 coaching formats.

Figure 8.2 Coaching Formats: Time and Intensity Factors

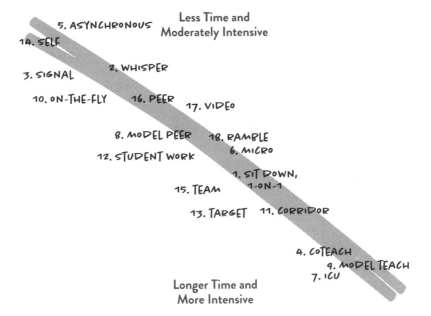

For teachers with students who have the highest needs, coach two or more times a week. For groups where student progress is on track, coach teachers about once a week. For groups of students who are exceeding expectations, coach about once every two weeks. Consider both individual coaching and small-group coaching as one coaching session.

Consider Novice Versus Expert Teachers

The final consideration to think about when using the 18 coaching formats is whether the teacher is new to the profession, struggling, or an expert teacher. Select the coaching format to match the needs of the teacher you're coaching. Some struggling and novice teachers benefit from Sit Down, 1-on-1 Coach; ICU; Coteach Coach; Model Teach Coach; Whisper Coach; and Signal Coach. Likewise, introspective and highly skilled teachers often do well with Asynchronous Coach, Self-Coach, Peer Coach, and Ramble Coach. Matheson (2019) identified ramble coaching as a model where the teacher and coach "walk and talk," or ramble. It's a very reflective model that is often leisurely and nondirected. It works well if the teacher easily vocalizes their thinking.

We recommend a few coaching structures for *all* teachers. These include Corridor Coach, Student Work Coach, Target Coach, and Team Coach. With Corridor Coach, you need more than one adult to conduct the coaching. Two or more people observe live instruction. Then the teacher and coach step into the hallway for a brief coaching conversation while another observer takes over the class. After a 5- to 10-minute coaching conversation, the teacher returns to take back their class. Most teachers who experience this format respond positively; in particular, they appreciate the immediate feedback and recommendations they can use right away. That said, this structure works best for the more self-confident teacher, not those who return to class overly anxious about the hallway critique. Also, this process is effective for training coaches or leaders who observe hallway conversations between a coach and a teacher or use the corridor analysis to gain interrater reliability on an observation protocol or instrument.

With Student Work Coach, the coach uses samples of student work or other student data for coaching teachers individually or in teams—another model suitable for all teachers. The coach leads the teacher in analyzing levels of thinking in student work or assignment questions, writing samples, photographic or videotaped evidence, lab write-ups, student portfolios, and so on. The coach leads the conversation, and the teacher sets goals based on the student work review. This approach easily combines with several other coaching formats.

If you focus coaching relentlessly on a single practice—academic, instructional, curricular, social-emotional, or other—you'll have the essence of Target Coach, a model that works well with almost all teachers. In this structure, you only coach the target practice until it's fully implemented; that is, it occurs 80 percent or more of the time requested. Disregard other feedback until the teacher has mastered the targeted practice. This process is powerful for implementing best practices for an entire school, department, grade level, or program. The coach provides feedback to whole groups or individuals.

Another format that works with most teacher teams is Team Coach. The coach leads group coaching (Skiffington & Zeus, 2000) or sets up structures, observation protocols, or data analysis questions so the team can coach itself. Teams consist of grade levels, departments, leadership teams, or affinity groups. The teams observe, coach, and teach one another. The teams analyze one another's student data and set goals for students and the team. This cycle of observing and providing one another with feedback repeats regularly. This is an ideal coaching format for a professional learning community (PLC); PLCs were first identified in the research as teacher learning formats (Little, 1993).

Figure 8.3 shows a continuum, from novice teacher to expert, and suggests how the 18 coaching formats might apply, given teachers' varied skill sets and experience.

Figure 8.3 Coaching Formats:
Novice Versus Expert Teachers

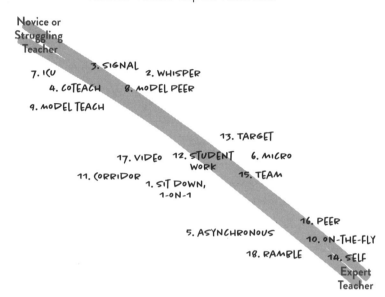

That Crucial Skill—Listening

Excellent listening skills are vital to coaching. We've noticed that the most remarkable coaches never stop working on their listening skills. It behooves any coach to read and learn as much as possible about this significant coaching asset. That said, in the guidelines that follow, we've boiled down some of the most valuable ideas about solid listening.

Quiet your inner voice. When listening, most of us are making a mental counterclaim or rebuttal while the person is speaking. It's hard to stop this practice completely, but try to calm that voice (Dumbro et al., 2020). Think to yourself something like "That's a fine point you just thought of, but pause it for now" or "Let's hear the teacher completely before continuing that thought."

Listen for generalities. When a teacher uses terms like *every-one, anybody, the school, these students, the administration,* or *the district,* that's a cue to pause and ask for clarification (Costa et al., 2016). Ask, "Who said that?" "Do you mean every single student?" "Who at the district office required that?" Sometimes, this helps you problem solve with the person. Other times, the generalization may signal a flaw in the teacher's critical thinking. Either way, listening for vague terminology helps you and the teacher be more precise and think more clearly.

Identify lingo or professional jargon. Over the years, we've learned that people make all sorts of assumptions about terms we hear all the time. It's a good idea to pause occasionally and clarify jargon so everyone in the discussion maintains the same under-standing. We've been repeatedly surprised at the extreme differ-ences in educator understanding of terms like *potential, skills, mastery, unique population, analysis,* and so on. If the stakes are high and talk is essential, work to agree on common terms.

Use wait time. When a teacher stops talking, count in your head "one-one thousand, two-one thousand, three-one thousand" before you start speaking. You're using and modeling wait time. The teacher will often begin speaking again during your pause. In fact, they often get to the heart of the matter at these moments.

Ask for more. Another strategy to get at core explanations is to ask, "What else?" or "Anything more?" when a teacher finishes. If there's time and a teacher is angry or frustrated, asking them to add to their comments helps them "get it all out." You can move on to problem solving or another tactic, once they've let all the steam out of their frustration.

Acknowledge. A primary characteristic of adult learners is that they want recognition of their unique experiences (Knowles et al., 2020). One of the best ways to do this is to *acknowledge* (Aguilar, 2013; Saphier et al., 2018). To help the teacher focus on the issue at hand, explain that you understand their concerns; their points of disagreement; and their descriptions of their unique circumstances, curriculum, or students. Validating a teacher's perspective can go a long way in fostering greater collaboration with you in a coaching session. We cannot overstate this point: *you need to verbally acknowledge their concerns, elaborate on their details if needed, summarize what you heard them state, and let them know you're trying to comprehend their point of view.* You don't need to agree with something you know is inaccurate or with a point you strongly disagree with, but do work to recognize their perspective on the issue.

Remove distractions. Try to get eye to eye with the person. Fully face them. Stop looking at your phone or computer during a coaching conversation.

Check your understanding. When teachers talk, you might need to clarify their remarks (Costa et al., 2016). Tell them you want to paraphrase or summarize what you heard. Say something similar to this: "It sounds like _____." "What I hear you saying is _____." "You're saying the problem is _____." Pause after your summary, and wait for them to clarify or confirm your understanding. When wrapping up a coaching session, ask the teacher to summarize their takeaways; this is your chance to see if the two of you are on the same page regarding what will happen next.

Find patterns, themes, or threads. Are there language patterns in the teacher's speech? Do they describe issues *visually* and make comments such as "I see the big picture" or "That's hard to visualize"? Perhaps they say, "I like the feel of that," "That's touching," "I get a pit in my stomach," or "That's a warm idea," suggesting they use a lot of kinesthetic metaphors. When you recognize such a trend, you're identifying a pattern in their metaphorical use of language and their thinking. Once you find it, borrow their preferences and use similar thematic language to make your point or move their thinking or practice forward (Costa et al., 2016). *Metaphor* in Arabic means "loan" (Al-Jurjani & Ritter, 1954). In this instance, the teacher is "loaning" you their metaphorical thinking, which you can then use to establish rapport with them. This strategy increases the likelihood that they will really hear you and improve their learning. Listen closely, and you'll find that a person's language is a symphony of metaphors.

The second benefit of identifying language patterns, other than metaphors, is that it helps you focus on the solutions the teacher may need. For example, are they doing more work than the students? A teacher might avoid talking about independent practice or stress how exhausted they are while the students still maintain a ton of energy. Are they focused on issues they *can* control? The teacher might only discuss factors influencing student learning that are outside their domain of control. This kind of listening may provide hints of where to offer suggestions.

Watch body language. Is the teacher covering their mouth, looking at the floor constantly, or fidgeting a lot? This body language communicates that they may be withholding something—or they could just be covering up bad breath. Either way, it's a good idea to probe by asking, "What's on your mind as we talk about this?" or "How are you hearing this feedback?" Such questions may surface unstated ideas.

Another common issue to look for is congruence between body language and spoken words (Aguilar, 2016; Costa et al., 2016; Shapiro, 2015; Smutny, 2019). If the teacher mentions they're enthusiastic about something, yet they sit slumped in their chair, are near tears, and have their arms crossed, they're sending mixed messages. Instead of pointing out the contradictory signals, try a general check-in: "What's exciting about that idea to you?" or "You say you're eager to do that; what's that about?" All that body language you noted could indicate they're really not excited, or it could mean they're in some kind of physical or psychological pain. They may be excited about the idea, but their body is just not showing enthusiasm at the moment. Either way, a general check-in is your chance to work with either scenario.

Interrupt when need be. In coaching, appropriate interruption is warranted. Sometimes the teacher loses their train of thought as they speak and forgets their point. Sometimes *you* forget the main point of the teacher's talk. At times, the conversation needs to return to work issues that the two of you control. Occasionally, a moment arises in the conversation for you to interject a solid suggestion or two, something the teacher entirely overlooked. These are all great places to consider interrupting the talk and shifting the focus back to the goal of the conversation. After all, coaching is a conversation with a goal. Therefore, ensure the majority of the coaching time is related to that goal.

Appendix A
The Research Behind Young's Apps

Young's Apps have a bit of history behind them. We hammered out the initial four approaches in our work with WestEd's Coach for Success program (WestEd, 2016), a framework that harkens back to the seven curriculum implementation conferences outlined by Madeline Hunter (1978, 1980). Eventually, we boiled the approaches down to four apps. First, we learned the power of switching between the more instructional coaching approach and the more reflective approach according to the teacher's needs—a direct application of Hersey and Blanchard's situational leadership theory (Northouse, 2022). Next, some of our favorite authors published coaching models based on situational leadership theory (whether they stated that up front or not). Finally, several writers and researchers advocated moving among various types of conversations for different individuals and contexts (Aguilar, 2013; Bloom et al., 2005; Costa et al., 2016; Marzano et al., 2013; Villani, 2009), which is an example of differentiated coaching and situational leadership. Hattie summarized a massive body of research on feedback to students that supported our belief in precise feedback with actionable follow-up steps (Hattie & Clarke, 2019).

The Research Undergirding the Framework

The notion of brainstorming ideas in feedback conversations for adults received support from the research on adult learning theory (Knowles et al., 2020) and our favorite Harvard researchers Stone and Heen (2014), who advocated brainstorming with adults, which is key to our approach. This process also addresses two adult learner needs: respecting their experience and providing choices (Knowles et al., 2020). We also credit Stone and Heen for our idea of opening with Positive Descriptive Appreciation (PDA), which aligns with Hattie's research on effective praise (Hattie & Clarke, 2019).

Several sources advocated gaining a commitment to action in the coaching conversation (Hattie & Clarke, 2019; Stone & Heen, 2014; WestEd, 2016). Hattie and others helped us recenter coaching on student outcomes (Hasbrouck, 2016; Hasbrouck & Denton, 2007). Goal-setting research informed our inclusion of the verbal summary at the end of the coaching conversation (Dweck, 2016; Morisano, 2013; Saphier, 2017; Saphier et al., 2018). Finally, overarching influences were the multiple studies on the power of both positive and frank, critical feedback (Anderson, 2014; Fishbach & Finkelstein, 2020; Fishbach et al., 2010; Fong et al., 2018; Hargrove, 2008; Killion, 2019; Zenger & Folkman, 2014). For these reasons, we're strong advocates of both instructional and reflective coaching.

Here is an example of how one coach deployed the first coaching app, the PDA:

> Saul, your students were so fortunate to have your annotated model of the math equations. Look, I took pictures of it on your whiteboard. I also grabbed a couple shots of it copied in student notes. Great job on planning that event for students during the lesson. Have you always color-coded the model like that? *(The teacher talks a bit about why they did the colored highlighting.)* Taking time

to model the operation before students do it on their own increases the chance they will understand its use more quickly. It is an excellent example of meeting the instructional goal set by the math department. Students need that kind of model at every single math block.

With that same teacher, the coach went on to deliver the second app, the Mini-Reflect. Here is how that sounded:

With a slight adjustment, the students could have demonstrated their thinking through writing during the lesson. What are some ways, in that same lesson, they could have written justifications for their answers? *(The teacher and coach generate three or four ideas, including writing on whiteboards.)* Great! Which one of those strategies will students do next time? *(The teacher selects written explanations on marker boards.)* Perfect. I'll look for students to be writing justifications on their whiteboards the next time I'm conducting weekly walkthroughs. Will you summarize our discussion? *(The teacher provides a brief recap of the conversation and their commitment.)*

Figure A.1 offers a visual summary of the research and theories supporting the use of the coaching apps.

Figure A.1   The Research Behind Young's Apps

RESEARCH SUPPORTS THE POSITIVE
FEEDBACK STRUCTURE OF STONE AND
HEEN'S POSITIVE DESCRIPTIVE
APPRECIATION (2014) AND HATTIE'S
FINDINGS ON EFFECTIVE PRAISE
(HATTIE & CLARKE, 2019).

HATTIE AND OTHERS RECOMMEND
CENTERING ON STUDENT OUTCOMES
(HASBROUCK, 2016; HASBROUCK &
DENTON, 2007; HATTIE & CLARKE, 2019).

BRAINSTORMING
IDEAS APPLIES
ADULT LEARNING
THEORY BY
RESPECTING
ADULTS'
EXPERIENCES AND
PROVIDING CHOICES
(KNOWLES ET AL.,
2020).

STONE AND HEEN
ADVOCATE
BRAINSTORMING
IN FEEDBACK AS
WELL (2014).

SWITCHING BETWEEN
INSTRUCTIONAL
AND REFLECTIVE
APPROACHES IS AN
APPLICATION OF
HERSEY AND
BLANCHARD'S
SITUATIONAL THEORY
(NORTHOUSE, 2022)
AND THE
FINDINGS OF
SEVERAL AUTHORS
& RESEARCHERS
(AGUILAR, 2013;
BLOOM ET AL., 2005;
COSTA ET AL., 2016;
MARZANO ET AL.,
2013; VILLANI,
2009). THIS
MOVEMENT
ADDRESSES
CHANGE THEORY
AS WELL (HALL &
HORD, 2019).

SEVERAL SOURCES
RECOMMEND
GAINING A
COMMITMENT TO
ACTION IN THE
COACHING
CONVERSATION
(HATTIE & CLARKE,
2019; STONE & HEEN,
2014; WESTED, 2016).

YOUNG'S 4 COACHING APPS

App	Begin Conversation	Mid-Conversation	End Conversation
PDA App (Positive Descriptive Appreciation) Start with PDA. Then, select App 1, 2, or 3 below.	State Positive Student Outcomes	Ask Questions About the Outcomes Connect to Best Practices, the Research Base, or the Schoolwide Focus	Encourage Continuation
1. Mini-Reflect App Go here with minor issues and briefer conversations.	State Students' Missed Opportunity	Discuss Ideas to Solve the Student Problem Get Commitment to One Solution	Set Time to See Implementation Get a Summary
2. Major-Reflect App Go here when the teacher is highly reflective and possesses a large bank of strategies.	Ask General Questions About Student Outcomes	Ask Specific Questions to Analyze the Data	Ask Questions for a Plan of Action Get a Summary
3. Instruct App Go here for a significant missed opportunity.	State Students' Major Missed Opportunity & Its Significance	Teach the Practice Needed	Set Time to See Implementation Get a Summary

MULTIPLE RESEARCHERS AND
AUTHORS COMMUNICATE THE
POWER OF PROVIDING POSITIVE
AND CRITICAL FEEDBACK
(ANDERSON, 2014; FISHBACH &
FINKELSTEIN, 2020; FISHBACH ET
AL., 2010; FONG ET AL., 2018;
HARGROVE, 2008; KILLION, 2019;
ZENGER & FOLKMAN, 2014).

GOAL-SETTING RESEARCH INFORMS
THE INCLUSION OF A VERBAL SUMMARY
AT THE END OF THE COACHING
CONVERSATION (MORISANO, 2013;
SAPHIER ET AL., 2018).

Appendix B
Tools for Tracking and Scripting

The artifacts that follow are a collection of formats and systems for tracking the coaching progress. When we coach coaches and administrators, they're required to set up a system for monitoring their progress and the effect of coaching on teacher practices and student outcomes. Some people prefer the feel of paper, whereas others prefer high-tech solutions.

Tracking

Sheena Alaiasa, named Middle School Principal of the Year in 2014 by the National Association of Secondary School Principals, received coaching from Keith and kept coaching files in the paper files shown in Figure B.1. The colorful folders sat on a credenza near the office door and served as a visual reminder to complete scheduled weekly coaching. Sheena eventually transitioned to keeping her files on a tablet.

Noah Leavitt, a principal in San Diego, California, used a word-processing file to log teacher coaching. The sample in Figure B.2 shows the teacher making progress with student engagement.

Scripting

Figure B.3 provides an outline for how we typically set up our paper to script in the classroom.

Figure B.1   Sample Coaching Logs in Paper Folders

Figure B.2 Sample Coaching Log

Teacher: Reynolds, 2nd grade

Date	Positive Descriptive Appreciation	Mini-reflect; Major-reflect; Instruct Apps	Coaching Format	Next Steps/Goals	Timeline By When
9/6	Ss get effective Explain & Model	Student Engagement Missed opportunity	Sit Down Coach	Have students reply in complete thoughts, and during the We Do, have them come up with own answers.	One Week
9/13			Team Coach	PLC: Impact Schedule; ELD; Writing Calendar	
9/16			Team Coach	PLC: Impact Schedule; ELD; Writing	
9/20			Team Coach	PLC: Lesson Planning; Lesson Study	
9/21	Ss get effective Explain & Model	Student Engagement missed	Sit Down Coach	A-B Partners use complete sentences; make participation mandatory	One Week
9/23	S Practice is solid	Student Engagement	Whisper	Live during a walkthrough whisper coached and provided a mini-demo on making engagement required	
9/27	S Engagement	No critique	Sit Down	Agreed to continue; made a plan for reminders to continue	Next Week
9/30			Team Coach	PLC: Lesson Planning	

Figure B.3 Tips for Setting Up Scripting Paper

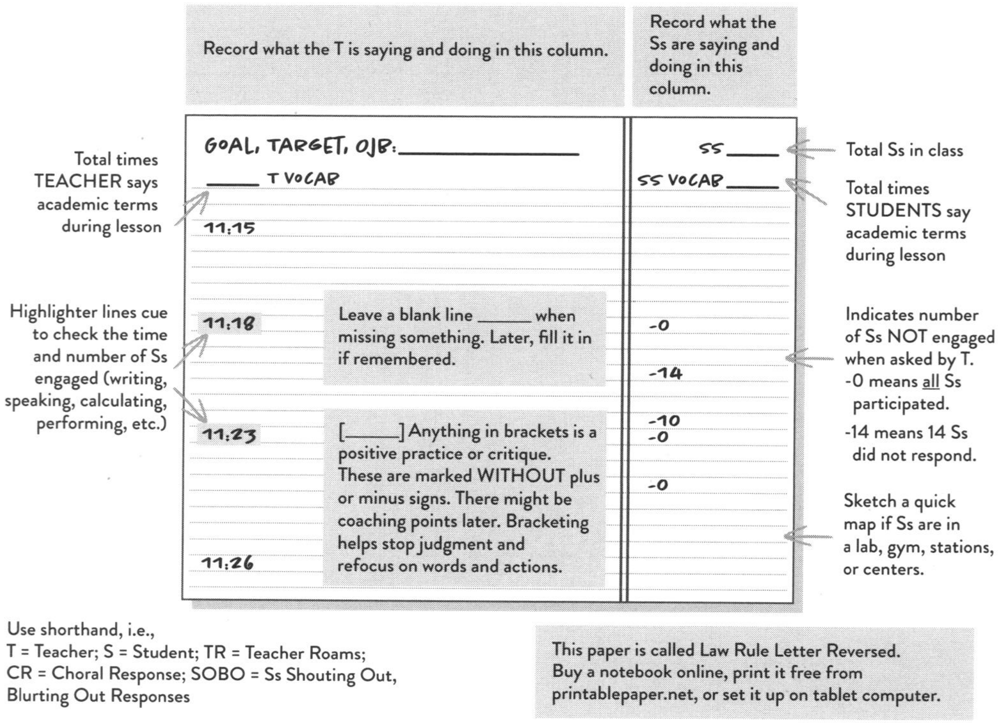

Record what the T is saying and doing in this column.

Record what the Ss are saying and doing in this column.

GOAL, TARGET, OBJ. _____	_____ Ss
T VOCAB _____	_____ Ss VOCAB
11:15	
11:18	-0
11:23	-14
	-10
	-0
11:26	-0

Total Ss in class

Total times STUDENTS say academic terms during lesson

Indicates number of Ss NOT engaged when asked by T.
-0 means all Ss participated.
-14 means 14 Ss did not respond.

Sketch a quick map if Ss are in a lab, gym, stations, or centers.

Total times TEACHER says academic terms during lesson

Highlighter lines cue to check the time and number of Ss engaged (writing, speaking, calculating, performing, etc.)

Leave a blank line _____ when missing something. Later, fill it in if remembered.

[_____] Anything in brackets is a positive practice or critique. These are marked WITHOUT plus or minus signs. There might be coaching points later. Bracketing helps stop judgment and refocus on words and actions.

This paper is called Law Rule Letter Reversed. Buy a notebook online, print it free from printablepaper.net, or set it up on tablet computer.

Use shorthand, i.e.,
T = Teacher; S = Student; TR = Teacher Roams;
CR = Choral Response; SOBO = Ss Shouting Out, Blurting Out Responses

References

Aguilar, E. (2013). *The art of coaching: Effective strategies for school transformation.* Jossey-Bass.

Aguilar, E. (2016). *The art of coaching teams: Building resilient communities that transform schools.* Jossey-Bass.

Alexander, M. (2020). *The new Jim Crow: Mass incarceration in the age of colorblindness.* New Press.

Al-Jurjani, A., & Ritter, H. (Eds.). (1954). *The mysteries of eloquence.* Government Press.

Allen, D., & Eve, A. (1968). Microteaching. *Theory into Practice, 7*(5), 181–185.

Almeida, M. F. (2020). *Aveyan & Addyn's very good day* [Unpublished manuscript].

Anderson, C. (2014). *Your employees want the negative feedback you hate to give: The surprising collapse of motivation in the modern workplace because employers are too nice.* CreateSpace.

Anderson, E., & Buchko, K. J. (2016). Giving negative feedback to millennials. *Management Research Review, 39*(6), 692–705.

Anderson, L. W., Krathwohl, D. R., & Bloom, B. S. (2001). *A taxonomy for learning, teaching, and assessing: A revision of Bloom's Taxonomy of educational objectives.* Longman.

Arbinger Institute. (2016). *The outward mindset: Seeing beyond ourselves.* Berrett-Koehler.

Armor, D., Conroy-Oseguera, P., Cox, M., King, N., McDonnell, L., Pascal, A., Pauly, E., & Zellman, G. (1976). *Analysis of the school preferred reading programs in selected Los Angeles minority schools.* Rand Corporation.

Ashford, S. J., & Tsui, A. S. (1991). Self-regulation for managerial effectiveness: The role of active feedback seeking. *Academy of Management Journal, 34*(2), 251–280.

Bailey, B. (2011). *Managing emotional mayhem: The five steps for self-regulation.* Loving Guidance.

Bailey, B. (2015). *Conscious discipline: Building resilient classrooms.* Loving Guidance.

Bambrick-Santoyo, P. (2019). *Driven by data 2.0: A practical guide to improve instruction.* Jossey-Bass.

Beck, I. L., McKeown, M. G., & Kucan, L. (2013). *Bringing words to life* (2nd ed.). Guilford.

Bilmes, J. (2012). *Beyond behavior management: The six life skills children need to thrive in today's world* (2nd ed.). Redleaf Press.

Bloom, G., Castagna, C., Moir, E., & Warren, B. (Eds.). (2005). *Blended coaching: Skills and strategies to support principal development.* Corwin.

Bocchino, R. (1999). *Emotional literacy: To be a different kind of smart.* Corwin.

Brady, S. T., Cohen, G. L., Jarvis, S. N., & Walton, G. M. (2020). A brief social-belonging intervention in college improves adult outcomes for Black Americans. *Science Advances, 6*(18).

Brewer, J. (2017). *The craving mind: From cigarettes to smartphones to love: Why we get hooked and how we can break bad habits.* Yale University Press.

Briggs, T. H. (1928). Sarcasm. *School Review, 36*(9), 685–695.

Buckingham, M., & Goodall, A. (2019, March–April). The feedback fallacy. *Harvard Business Review.*

Burns, J. M. (1978). *Leadership.* Harper & Row.

Chen, Z., Lam, W., & Zhong, J. A. (2007). Leader-member exchange and member performance: A new look at individual-level negative feedback-seeking behavior and team-level empowerment climate. *Journal of Applied Psychology, 92*(1), 202–212.

Chhokar, J. S., Brodbeck, F. C., & House, R. J. (Eds.). (2019). *Culture and leadership across the world: The GLOBE book of in-depth studies of 25 societies* (2nd ed.). Psychology Press.

Clark, S. (2013). *Feedback that works for nonprofit organizations.* Center for Creative Leadership.

Cohen, G. L., Garcia, J., Apfel, N., & Master, A. (2006). Reducing the racial achievement gap: A social-psychological intervention. *Science, 313*(5791), 1307–1310.

Costa, A. L., Garmston, R. J., Hayes, C., & Ellison, J. (2016). *Cognitive coaching: Developing self-directed leaders and learners* (3rd ed). Rowman & Littlefield.

Covey, S. R. (2020). *7 Habits of highly effective people: Powerful lessons in personal change* (4th ed.). Simon & Schuster.

Cowan, N. (2000). The magical number 4 in short-term memory: A reconsideration of mental storage capacity. *Behavioral and Brain Sciences, 24*(1), 87–185.

Curwin, R. L., Mendler, A. N., & Mendler, B. D. (2008). *Discipline with dignity: New challenges, new solutions.* ASCD.

Danielson, C. (2007). *Enhancing professional practice: A framework for teaching* (2nd ed.). ASCD.

Darling-Hammond, L., Flook, L., Cook-Harvey, C., Barron, B., & Osher, D. (2020). Implications for the educational practice of the science of learning and development. *Applied Developmental Science, 24*(2), 97–140.

Delpit, L. (2012). *"Multiplication is for white people": Raising expectations for other people's children.* New Press.

DeLuca, V., & Voits, T. (2022). Bilingual experience affects white matter integrity across the lifespan. *Neuropsychologia, 169*, 108191.

DeRuvo, S. L. (2010). *The essential guide to RTI: An integrated, evidence-based approach.* Jossey-Bass.

Dewey, J. (2019). *How we think* (Revised and expanded ed.). Wadsworth. (Original work published 1909).

Di Michele Lalor, A. (2020, October 22). *3 Steps for developing an asset-based approach to teaching.* Edutopia. www.edutopia.org/article/3-steps-developing-asset-based-approach-teaching

Divinyi, J. (2010). *Good kids, difficult behavior: A guide to what works and what doesn't.* B. Jain. (Original work published 1997).

Donohoo, J., & Katz, S. (2019). What drives collective efficacy? *Educational Leadership, 76*(6), 24–29.

Dumbro, A. L., Jablon, J., & Stetson, C. (2020). *Coaching with powerful interactions: How to connect with children to extend their learning* (2nd ed.). National Association for the Education of Young Children.

Dweck, C. (2016). *Mindset: The new psychology of success* (2nd ed.). Random House.

Eberhardt, J. L. (2019). *Biased: Uncovering the hidden prejudice that shapes what we see, think, and do.* Penguin Books.

Emdin, C. (2016). *For white folks who teach in the hood... and the rest of y'all too: Reality pedagogy and urban education.* Beacon.

Esquivel, K., Elam, E., Paris, J., & Tafoya, M. (2020). *The role of equity and diversity in early childhood education.* Open Educational Resources Publication of the College of the Canyons [California]. https://childdevelopment.org/docs/default-source/pdfs/role-equity-and-diversityenglish-2-8-20.pdf?sfvrsn=3bf4a9a6_2

Fay, J. (2011). *Creating a love and logic school culture.* Love and Logic Press.

Feldman, J. (2018). *Grading for equity: What it is, why it matters, and how it can transform schools and classrooms.* Corwin.

Fiorella, L., & Mayer, R. E. (2016). Effects of observing the instructor draw diagrams on learning from multimedia lessons. *Journal of Educational Psychology, 108*, 528–546.

Fishbach, A., Eyal, T., & Finkelstein, S. R. (2010). How positive and negative feedback motivate goal pursuit. *Social and Personality Psychology Compass, 4*(8), 517–530.

Fishbach, A., & Finkelstein, S. R. (2020). How feedback influences persistence, disengagement, and change in goal pursuit. In H. Aarts & A. Elliot (Eds.), *Goal-directed behavior: The concept of action in psychology.* Routledge.

Fisher, D., Frey, N., & Hattie, J. (2016). *Visible learning for literacy: Implementing the practices that work best to accelerate student learning.* Corwin.

Fisher, D., Frey, N., & Hattie, J. (2017). *Visible learning for mathematics: What works best to optimize student learning.* Corwin.

Fong, C. J., Patall, E. A., Vasquez, A. C., & Stautberg, S. (2018). A meta-analysis of negative feedback on intrinsic motivation. *Educational Psychology Review, 31*(1), 121–162.

Garet, M. S., Heppen, J. B., Walters, K., Parkinson, J., Smith, T. M., Song, M., Garrett, R., Yang, R., & Borman, G. D. (2016). *Focusing on mathematical knowledge: The impact of content-intensive teacher professional development* (NCEE 2016-4010). National Center for Education Evaluation and Regional Assistance, Institute of Education Sciences, U.S. Department of Education.

Gawande, A. (2011). *The checklist manifesto: How to get things right*. Picador.

Geary, J. (2011). *I is an other: The secret life of metaphor and how it shapes the way we see the world*. HarperCollins.

Gilbert, D. (2007). *Stumbling on happiness*. Vintage.

Gilovich, T., & Savitsky, K. (1999). The spotlight effect and the illusion of transparency. *Current Directions in Psychological Science, 8*(6), 165–168.

Good, C., Aronson, J., & Inzlicht, M. (2003). Improving adolescents' standardized test performance: An intervention to reduce the effects of stereotype threat. *Journal of Applied Developmental Psychology, 24*(6), 645–662.

Gordon, T., & Burch, N. (2003). *Teacher effectiveness training: The program proven to help teachers bring out the best in students of all ages*. Three Rivers Press.

Gottman, J. M., & Silver, N. (2015). *The seven principles for making marriage work: A practical guide from the country's foremost relationship expert*. Harmony Books.

Goyer, J. P., Garcia, J., Purdie-Vaughns, V., Binning, K. R., Cook, J. E., Reeves, S. L., Apfel, N., Taborsky-Barba, S., Sherman, D. K., & Cohen, G. L. (2017). Self-affirmation facilitates minority middle schoolers' progress along college trajectories. *Proceedings of the National Academy of Sciences, 114*(29), 7594–7599.

Grant, V. J., Robinson, T., Catena, H., Eppich, W., & Cheng, A. (2018). Difficult debriefing situations: A toolbox for simulation educators. *Medical Teacher, 40*(7), 703–712.

Gregory, A., Hafen, C. A., Ruzek, E., Mikami, A. Y., Allen, J. P., & Pianta, R. C. (2016). Closing the racial discipline gap in classrooms by changing teacher practice. *School Psychology Review, 45*(2), 171–191.

Hall, G., & Hord, S. (2019). *Implementing change: Patterns, principles, and potholes* (5th ed.). Pearson.

Hammond, Z. (2015). *Culturally responsive teaching and the brain: Promoting authentic engagement and rigor among culturally and linguistically diverse students*. Corwin.

Hargrove, R. (2008). *Masterful coaching* (3rd ed.). Wiley.

Harless, J. H. (1986). Guiding performance with job aids. In M. Smith (Ed.), *Introduction to performance technology* (pp. 106–124). International Society for Performance Improvement.

Harmin, M., & Toth, M. (2006). *Inspiring active learning: A complete handbook for today's teachers*. ASCD.

Hasbrouck, J. (2016). Student-focused coaching. *Theory into Practice, 56*(1), 21–28.

Hasbrouck, J., & Denton, C. A. (2007). Student-focused coaching: A model for reading coaches. *The Reading Teacher, 60*, 690–693.

Hattie, J. (2012). *Visible learning for teachers: Maximizing impact on learning.* Routledge.

Hattie, J. (2022). Hattie ranking: 252 Influences and effect sizes related to student achievement. Visible Learning. https://visible-learning.org/hattie-ranking-influences-effect-sizes-learning-achievement/

Hattie, J., & Clarke, S. (2019). *Visible learning: Feedback.* Routledge.

Head Start. (2020, December 15). *Professional development: Practice-based coaching.* Early Childhood Learning and Knowledge Center.

Helms, J. E. (2019). *A race is a nice thing to have: A guide to being a white person or understanding the white persons in your life* (3rd ed.). Cognella.

Hersey, P., & Blanchard, K. H. (1969). Life-cycle theory of leadership. *Training and Development Journal, 23*, 26–34.

Honsinger, C., & Brown, M. H. (2019). Preparing trauma-sensitive teachers: Strategies for teacher educators. *Teacher Educators' Journal, 12*, 129–152.

House, R. J., Dorfman, P. W., Javidan, M., Hanges, P. J., & Sully de Luque, M. F. (2014). *Strategic leadership across cultures: GLOBE study of CEO leadership behavior and effectiveness in 24 countries.* SAGE Publications.

Hunter, D. (2015). *Building a movement to end the new Jim Crow: An organizing guide.* Hyrax.

Hunter, M. (1978). *A clinical theory of instruction.* TIP Publications.

Hunter, M. (1980). Six types of supervisory conferences. *Educational Leadership, 37*(5), 408–412.

Institute on Trauma and Trauma-Informed Care (ITTIC). (2022). *What is trauma-informed care?* University at Buffalo School of Social Work. http://socialwork.buffalo.edu/social-research/institutes-centers/institute-on-trauma-and-trauma-informed-care/what-is-trauma-informed-care.html

Jackson, R. R. (2018). *Never work harder than your students and other principles of great teaching* (2nd ed.). ASCD.

James, T., & Shephard, B. (2001). *Presenting magically.* Crown House.

John, O. P., Naumann, L. P., & Soto, C. J. (2008). Paradigm shift to the integrative Big Five trait taxonomy: History, measurement, and conceptual issues. In O. P. John, R. W. Robins, & L. A. Pervin (Eds.), *Handbook of personality: Theory and research* (pp. 114–158). Guilford.

Joyce, B. R., & Showers, B. (1982). The coaching of teaching. *Educational Leadership, 40*(1), 4–10.

Joyce, B. R., & Showers, B. (2002). *Student achievement through staff development.* ASCD.

Joyce, B. R., Weil, M., & Calhoun, E. (2017). *Models of teaching* (9th ed.). Pearson.

Kee, K., Anderson, K., Dearing, V., Harris, E., & Shuster, F. (2010). *Results coaching: The new essential for school leaders.* Corwin.

Kendi, I. X. (2019). *How to be an antiracist.* One World.

Killion, J. (2019). *The feedback process: Transforming feedback for professional learning* (2nd ed). Learning Forward.

Kim, L., Jorg, V., & Klassen, R. M. (2019). A meta-analysis of the effects of teacher personality on teacher effectiveness and burnout. *Educational Psychology Review, 31*, 163–195.

Kimmerer, R. W. (2020). *Braiding sweetgrass: Indigenous wisdom, scientific knowledge, and the teachings of plants.* Milkweed.

Kleinfeld, J. (1975). Effective teachers of Eskimo and Indian students. *School Review, 83*, 301–344.

Kliesch, M., Becker, R., & Hervais-Adelman, A. (2022). Global and localized network characteristics of the resting brain predict and adapt to foreign language learning in older adults. *Scientific Reports, 12*(1), 3633.

Klockner, C. A., & Verplanken, B. (2019). Yesterday's habits preventing change for tomorrow? About the influence of automaticity on environmental behaviour. In L. Steg, A. van den Berg, & J. I. M. de Groot (Eds.), *Environmental psychology: An introduction* (2nd ed.) (pp. 238–250.). Wiley.

Knight, J. (2016). *Better conversations: Coaching ourselves and each other to be more credible, caring, and connected.* Corwin.

Knight, J. (2018). *The impact cycle: What instructional coaches should do to foster powerful improvement in teaching.* Corwin.

Knowles, M. S., Holton, E. F., III, Swanson, R. A., & Robinson, P. A. (2020). *The adult learner: The definitive classic in adult education and human resource development* (9th ed.). Routledge.

Kraft, M. A., Blazar, D., & Hogan, D. (2018). The effect of teacher coaching on instruction and achievement: A meta-analysis of the causal evidence. *Review of Educational Research, 88*(4), 547–588.

Ladson-Billings, G. (2021). *Culturally relevant pedagogy: Asking a different question.* Culturally Sustaining Pedagogies Series. Teachers College Press.

Laird, D. A. (1923). How the high school student responds to different incentives to work. *The Pedagogical Seminary, 30*(4), 357–365.

Learning Forward. (2010, August 31). *Ford Middle School: PD in action* [Video]. YouTube. www.youtube.com/watch?reload=9&v=T8F04iD4Yc8

Lemov, D. (2021). *Teach like a champion 3.0: 63 techniques that put students on the path to college.* Jossey-Bass.

Leong, K., Sung, A., Au, D., & Blanchard, C. (2021). A review of the trend of microlearning. *Journal of Work-Applied Management, 13*(1), 88–102.

Little, J. W. (1993). Professional community in comprehensive high schools: The two worlds of academic and vocational teachers. In J. Little & M. McLaughlin (Eds.), *Teacher's work: Individuals, colleagues, and contexts* (pp. 137–163). Teachers College Press.

Loewen, J. W. (2007). *Lies my teacher told me: Everything your American history textbook got wrong.* New Press.

Marzano, R. J. (2013). *Developing a passion for professional teaching: The Marzano teacher evaluation model.* Learning Sciences International.

Marzano, R. J., Simms, J. A., Roy, T., Heflebower, T., & Warrick, P. (2013). *Coaching classroom instruction.* Marzano Research Laboratory.

Matheson, R. (2019). In pursuit of teaching excellence: Outward and visible signs of inward and invisible grace. *Teaching in Higher Education, 25*(8), 909–925.

Mayer, R. E., & Anderson, R. B. (1991). Animations need narrations: An experimental test of a dual-coding hypothesis. *Journal of Educational Psychology, 83*(4), 484–490.

McCarney, S. B., Wunderlich, K. C., & House, S. N. (Ed.). (2014). *Pre-referral intervention manual: The most common learning and behavior problems encountered in the educational environment* (4th ed.). Hawthorne Education Services.

McGhee, H. (2021). *The sum of us: What racism costs everyone and how we can prosper together.* Profile Books.

McGonigal, K. (2015). *The upside of stress: Why stress is good for you and how to get good at it.* Random House.

Moran, M. C. (2007). *Differentiated literacy coaching: Scaffolding for student and teacher success.* ASCD.

Morisano, D. (2013). Goal setting in the academic arena. In E. A. Locke & G. Latham (Eds.), *New developments in goal setting and task performance* (pp. 495–506). Routledge.

Mueller, P. A., & Oppenheimer, D. M. (2014). The pen is mightier than the keyboard: Advantages of longhand over laptop note taking. *Psychological Science, 25*(6), 1159–1168.

Muhammad, G. (2020). *Cultivating genius: An equity framework for culturally and historically responsive literacy.* Scholastic.

Murphey, C., & D'Auria, J. (2021). *The influential school leaders: Inspiring teachers, students, and families through social and organizational psychology.* Routledge.

Narvaez, D., Halton, E., Collier, B., & Enderle, G. (Eds.). (2019). *Indigenous sustainable wisdom: First-Nation know-how for global flourishing.* Peter Lang.

Nasir, N. S., Cabana, C., Shreve, B., Woodbury, E., Louid, N., & Banks, J. A. (Eds.). (2014). *Mathematics for equity: A framework for successful practice.* Teachers College Press.

National Academies of Sciences, Engineering, and Medicine (NASEM). (2018). *How people learn II: Learners, contexts, and cultures.* National Academies Press.

National Association for the Education of Young Children (NAEYC). (2019). *Advancing equity in early childhood education: A position statement of the National Association for the Education of Young Children.* www.naeyc.org/resources/position-statements/equity

National Council on Teacher Quality (NCTQ). (2012). Teacher planning time. *TR3 Trends*. www.nctq.org/blog/TR3-Trends:-Teacher-Planning-Time#:~:text=Elementary%20school%20teachers%20in%20Tr3,does%20so%20for%20secondary%20teachers

Noddings, N. (2013). *Caring: A relational approach to ethics and moral education* (2nd ed.). University of California Press.

Northouse, P. G. (2022). *Leadership: Theory and practice* (9th ed.). Sage.

Ohno, T. (1988). *Toyota production system: Beyond large-scale production*. Taylor & Francis.

Ophir, E., Nass, C., & Wagner, A. D. (2009). Cognitive control in media multitaskers. *Proceedings of the National Academy of Sciences, 106*(37), 15583–15587.

Organisation for Economic Co-operation & Development (OECD). (2014a). *A teacher's guide to TALIS 2013: Teaching and learning international survey.*

Organisation for Economic Co-operation & Development (OECD). (2014b). *New insights from TALIS 2013: Teaching and learning in primary education.*

Parry, D. A., & Le Roux, D. B. (2021). "Cognitive control in media multitaskers" 10 years on: A meta-analysis. *Cyberpsychology: Journal of Psychosocial Research on Cyberspace, 15*(2), 1–26.

Patterson, K., Grenny, J., McMillan, R., & Switzler, A. (2012). *Crucial conversations: Tools for talking when stakes are high* (2nd ed.). McGraw-Hill.

Peper, R. J., & Mayer, R. E. (1986). Generative effects of note-taking during science lectures. *Journal of Educational Psychology, 78*(1), 34–38.

Posselt, J. R. (2020). *Equity in science: Representation, culture, and the dynamics of change in graduate education*. Stanford University Press.

Prescod-Weinstein, C. (2021). *The disordered cosmos: A journey into dark matter, spacetime, and dreams deferred*. Bold Type Books.

Reynolds, J., & Kendi, I. X. (2020). *Stamped: Racism, antiracism, and you*. Little, Brown.

Rigby, K. (2012). *Bullying interventions in schools: Six basic approaches*. Wiley-Blackwell.

Ritchart, R., Church, M., & Morrison, K. (2011). *Making thinking visible: How to promote engagement, understanding, and independence for all learners*. Jossey-Bass.

Rock, D. (2020). *Your brain at work, revised and updated: Strategies for overcoming distraction, regaining focus, and working smarter all day long* (2nd ed.). HarperCollins.

Saad, L. F. (2020). *Me and white supremacy: Combat racism, change the world, and become a good ancestor*. Sourcebooks.

saddestmonkey. (2020, September 1). Thank you teachers!!! [Online post]. Reddit. www.reddit.com/r/education/comments/ikfnf1/thank_you_teachers/

Santos, F. (2017, July). *How to defuse a child's tantrum with one question*. [Blog post]. https://aleteia.org/2017/05/01/how-to-diffuse-a-childs-tantrum-with-one-question

Saphier, J. (2017). *High expectations teaching: How we persuade students to believe and act on "Smart is something you can get."* Corwin.

Saphier, J., Haley Speca, M., & Gower, R. R. (2018). *The skillful teacher: Building your teaching skills* (7th ed.). Research for Better Teaching.

Saucier, G., & Goldberg, L. R. (1996). Evidence for the Big Five in analyses of familiar English personality adjectives. *European Journal of Personality, 10,* 61–77.

Schön, D. A. (1983). *The reflective practitioner: How professionals think in action.* Basic Books.

Seligman, M. E., & Csikszentmihalyi, M. (2014). Positive psychology: An introduction. *Flow and the Foundations of Positive Psychology, 279–298.*

Shalley, C. E., Hitt, M. A., & Zhou, J. (2015). Introduction: Integrating creativity, innovation, and entrepreneurship to enhance the organization's capability to navigate in the new competitive landscape. In C. E. Shalley, M. A. Hitt, & J. Zhou (Eds.), *The Oxford handbook for creativity, innovation, and entrepreneurship* (pp. 1–14). Oxford University Press.

Shapiro, M. (2015). *HBR guide to leading teams: Balance skills and styles, establish clear roles, promote healthy dissent.* Harvard Business Review Press.

Skiffington, S., & Zeus, P. (2000). *The complete guide to coaching at work.* McGraw-Hill.

Smith, R. (2004). *Conscious classroom management: Unlocking the secrets of great teaching.* Conscious Teaching Publications.

Smutny, M. (2019). *THRIVE: The facilitator's guide to radically inclusive meetings.* Civic Reinventions.

Snyder, P. A., Hemmeter, M. L., & Fox, L. (2015). Supporting implementation of evidence-based practices through practice-based coaching. *Topics in Early Childhood Special Education, 35*(3), 133–143.

Sprick, R. (2012). *Teacher's encyclopedia of behavior management: 100+ problems/100+ plans* (2nd ed.). Pacific Northwest Publishing.

Stanier, M. B. (2016). *The coaching habit: Say less, ask more & change the way you lead forever.* Box of Crayons Press.

Stone, D., & Heen, S. (2014). *Thanks for the feedback: The science and art of receiving feedback well.* Viking.

Sue, D. W. (2016). *Race talk and the conspiracy of silence: Understanding and facilitating difficult dialogues on race.* Wiley.

Sujansky, J. G., & Ferri-Reed, J. (2009). *Keeping the millennials: Why companies are losing billions in turnover to this generation—And what to do about it.* Wiley.

Sussman, R. W. (2014). *The myth of race: The troubling persistence of an unscientific idea.* Harvard University Press.

Tatum, B. D. (2017). *Why are all the Black kids sitting together in the cafeteria? Conversations about race* (2nd ed.). Basic Books.

Umejima, K., Ibaraki, T., Yamazaki, T., & Sakai, K. L. (2021). Paper notebooks vs. mobile devices: Brain activation differences during memory retrieval. *Frontiers in Behavioral Neuroscience, 15,* 1–11.

U.S. Department of Education Office for Civil Rights (USDoEOCR). (2014). *Civil rights data collection data snapshot: School discipline.* https://www2.ed.gov/about/offices/list/ocr/docs/crdc-discipline-snapshot.pdf

Van Velsor, E., McCauley, C. D., & Ruderman, M. N. (Eds.). (2010). *The Center for Creative Leadership handbook of leadership development* (3rd ed.). Jossey Bass & Center for Creative Leadership.

The Veterans of Hope Project. (2013). *The new Jim Crow study guide and call to action.* Author.

Villani, S. (2009). *Comprehensive mentoring programs for new teachers: Models of induction and support* (2nd ed.). WestEd.

Voits, T., Pliatsikas, C., Robson, H., & Rothman, J. (2020). Beyond Alzheimer's disease: Can bilingualism be a more generalized protective factor in neuro-degeneration? *Neuropsychologia, 147,* 107593.

Voits, T., Robson, H., Rothman, J., & Pliatsikas, C. (2022). The effects of bilingualism on hippocampal volume in aging bilinguals. *Brain Structure and Function, 227*(3), 979–994.

Von Bergen, C. W., Bressler, M. S., & Campbell, K. (2014). The sandwich feedback method: Not very tasty. *Journal of Behavioral Studies in Business, 7,* 1–13.

Wadhwa, A. (2016). *Restorative justice in urban schools: Disrupting the school-to-prison pipeline.* Routledge.

Walton, G. M., & Cohen, G. L. (2011). A brief social-belonging intervention improves academic and health outcomes of minority students. *Science, 331*(6023), 1447–1451.

Webb, N. L. (2002). *Alignment study in language arts, mathematics, science, and social studies of state standards and assessments for four states.* Council of Chief State School Officers.

Webb, N. L. (2007). Mathematics content specification in the age of assessment. In F. K. Lester Jr. (Ed.), *Second handbook of research on mathematics teaching and learning.* Information Age Publishing.

Webb, N. L. (2012, December). Content complexity for mathematics and science instructional planning. Presentation at Florida Center for Research in Science, Technology, Engineering, and Mathematics. Florida State University. Retrieved from http://facstaff.wcer.wisc.edu/normw/AERA%20Page1.htm

Weiner, B. (1974). *Achievement motivation and attribution theory.* General Learning Press.

Wenger, E. (1999). *Communities of practice: Learning, meaning, and identity.* Cambridge University Press.

WestEd. (2016, January). Coach for Success and Teach for Success training presented to Goodland Elementary School staff in Racine, Wisconsin [Workshop materials].

Willmore, J. (2018). *Job aids basics* (2nd ed.). ATD Press.

Wilson, M. B. (2012). *Interactive modeling: A powerful technique for teaching children.* Northeast Foundation for Children.

Wlodkowski, R. J. (1983). *Motivational opportunities for successful teaching* [Leader's guide]. Universal Dimensions.

Wood, W., Quinn, J. M., & Kashy, D. A. (2002). Habits in everyday life: Thought, emotion, and action. *Journal of Personality and Social Psychology, 83*(6), 1281–1297.

Yoon, J. H., Kang, M. Y., Jeung, D. Y., & Chang, S. J. (2017). Suppressing emotion and engaging with complaining customers at work related to experience of depression and anxiety symptoms: A nationwide cross-sectional study. *Industrial Health, 55*(3), 265–274.

Zenger, J., & Folkman, J. (2014, January 15). Your employees want the negative feedback you hate to give. *Harvard Business Review.* https://hbr.org/2014/01/your-employees-want-the-negative-feedback-you-hate-to-give

Index

The letter *f* following a page locator denotes a figure. In Practice vignettes are capitalized.

About the Authors

 **A. Keith Young** is an education coach, trainer, and writer. Keith was born and raised in the foothills of the Appalachian Mountains of northern Alabama. He studied to be an English teacher. After a short stint at seminary, he pivoted to teaching secondary students English and math for the U.S. government in Germany. In his first years of teaching, he developed a knack for leading and training colleagues. In addition, he was immersed in training and coaching from prominent educational leaders, including Jon Saphier, Louise Thomson, Ernie Stokowski, Robby Champion, Rick DuFour, and Robert Garmston. Eventually, Keith shifted full-time to training teachers and leading school improvement efforts at the school district level. Later, he became a principal, leading school turnaround work and regularly increasing student outcomes by double digits in Colorado, Puerto Rico, and Arizona. Along the way, Keith picked up several advanced education degrees.

Nowadays, Keith trains and coaches administrators, school leadership teams, and teacher coaches. As a trainer, he maintains a progressive philosophy and a teaching style that embraces the best of constructivism and direct instruction. As a coach, he's known for "telling it like it is" and using a blended coaching model. The schools Keith coaches across the United States and internationally produce significant increases in student outcomes, both academically and affectively.

Angela Bell Julien owns and manages Angela Bell Julien Publications & Consulting. She provides school leaders and teachers with practical implementation strategies in site leadership, instructional improvement, strategic cycles of inquiry for systemic improvement, and relationship building.

Angela was born in Phoenix, Arizona. She never planned on becoming a teacher, but her college majors in English and theater led her to the high school classroom, where she was profoundly changed by encounters with students who were lost in the system. Angela followed the work of William Glasser, Ted Sizer, Jon Saphier, Bruce Wellman, and others and quickly became a leader of her peers as department chair, peer evaluator, assistant principal for curriculum and instruction, and high school principal. All told, she spent close to 35 years working in high schools. Intrigued by the small learning communities movement, she molded the process into a pathway to provide equity, decrease dropout rates, and increase post–high school success for all students.

From 2008 to 2021, Angela served as a school and district improvement facilitator for WestEd, providing training, professional development, and technical assistance to support leadership, differentiated instruction, writing instruction, and student achievement improvement efforts for K–12 schools in Hawaii, Arizona, California, Nevada, Maryland, and Colorado. Angela also paints and writes poetry; she has three published books of illustrated poetry and prompted journals.

Tamarra Osborne is a project manager, trainer, and coach with WestEd, a national nonprofit in San Francisco, California. Born and raised in Oakland, California, she's one of five siblings and a first-generation college graduate. Deciding to stay close to a tight-knit family, she attended

California State University in Sacramento. Tamarra earned a degree in early childhood education, realizing a dream that began at age 16 when she started working with preschoolers for Oakland's Parks and Recreation Department. After a brief period teaching English in Japan, she launched her teacher leadership and early care career.

Tamarra's philosophy of early education favors students learning through experiences and using play to learn academics. After 10 years directing an innovative childcare center in California, Tamarra took her expertise to WestEd. At WestEd, she serves as the project manager for the Desired Results Training and Technical Assistance Project, which provides a groundbreaking statewide observational assessment of young learners.

Tamarra is known as an effervescent trainer and technical coach who sees the heart of a problem and provides sensible, warm-hearted solutions. Tamarra has a knack for technology proficiency and delivers training and coaching in multiple U.S. states, as well as in China. Her training topics include formative assessment, curriculum development, presentation skills, implicit bias, and educational technology. Tamarra is proud to be published in *Young Children* magazine from the National Association for the Education of Young Children.

Related ASCD Resources: Instructional Coaching

At the time of publication, the following resources were available (ASCD stock numbers in parentheses).

The Artisan Teaching Model for Instructional Leadership: Working Together to Transform Your School by Kenneth Baum and David Krulwich (#116041)

Building Teachers' Capacity for Success: A Collaborative Approach for Coaches and School Leaders by Pete Hall and Alisa A. Simeral (#109002)

The Coach Approach to School Leadership: Leading Teachers to Higher Levels of Effectiveness by Jessica Johnson, Shira Leibowitz, and Kathy Perret (#117025)

The Definitive Guide to Instructional Coaching: Seven Factors for Success by Jim Knight (#121006)

Educational Coaching: A Partnership for Problem Solving by Cathy A. Toll (#118027)

Evaluating Instructional Coaching: People, Programs, and Partnership by Sharon Thomas, Jim Knight, Michelle Harris, and Ann Hoffman (#122039)

Instructional Coaching in Action: An Integrated Approach That Transforms Thinking, Practice, and Schools by Ellen B. Eisenberg, Bruce P. Eisenberg, Elliott A. Medrich, and Ivan Charner (#117028)

Learning from Coaching: How do I work with an instructional coach to grow as a teacher? by Nina Morel (#SF114066)

Peer Coaching to Enrich Professional Practice, School Culture, and Student Learning by Pam Robbins (#115014)

For up-to-date information about ASCD resources, go to www.ascd.org. You can search the complete archives of *Educational Leadership* at www.ascd.org/el.

ASCD myTeachSource®

Download resources from a professional learning platform with hundreds of research-based best practices and tools for your classroom at http://myteachsource.ascd.org

For more information, send an email to member@ascd.org; call 1-800-933-2723 or 703-578-9600; send a fax to 703-575-5400; or write to Information Services, ASCD, 2800 Shirlington Rd., Suite 1001, Arlington, VA 22206 USA.

ascd
whole child

The ASCD Whole Child approach is an effort to transition from a focus on narrowly defined academic achievement to one that promotes the long-term development and success of all children. Through this approach, ASCD supports educators, families, community members, and policymakers as they move from a vision about educating the whole child to sustainable, collaborative actions.

The Instructional Coaching Handbook relates to the **engaged, supported,** and **challenged** tenets. *For more about the ASCD Whole Child approach, visit* **www.ascd.org/wholechild.**

WHOLE CHILD
TENETS

1 **HEALTHY**
Each student enters school healthy and learns about and practices a healthy lifestyle.

2 **SAFE**
Each student learns in an environment that is physically and emotionally safe for students and adults.

3 **ENGAGED**
Each student is actively engaged in learning and is connected to the school and broader community.

4 **SUPPORTED**
Each student has access to personalized learning and is supported by qualified, caring adults.

5 **CHALLENGED**
Each student is challenged academically and prepared for success in college or further study and for employment and participation in a global environment.